Port Vendres
Blanes
Costa Brava
Barcelona
Tarragona
Costa Dorada
Vinaroz
MINORCA
Costa del Azahar
Palma
MAJORCA
BALEARIC ISLANDS
cia
IBIZA
te
Costa Blanca

down the Spanish Coast

Philip Bristow
down the Spanish Coast

Nautical Publishing Company Limited

First published in Great Britain by
Nautical Publishing Company Limited
Nautical House, Lymington, Hampshire
2nd Edition 1976

ISBN 0 245 50996 8

By the same author

Bristow's Book of Yachts
Through the French Canals
Through the Belgian Canals
Through the Dutch Canals
Through the German Waterways
French Mediterranean Harbours
Round the Italian Coast

*Despite every effort to ensure that information given in this
book is accurate and up-to-date, it is regretted that neither author
nor publisher can accept responsibility for errors or omissions.*

Filmset and printed in Great Britain by
BAS Printers Limited, Wallop, Hampshire

To Emma

Acknowledgements

I am indebted to many Tourist Offices of the Spanish Government for the facts and figures that they have kindly made available and to the officials of the various Clubs Nautico for their help and guidance.

For the photographs in support of my own I have the pleasure of acknowledging the following: Eileen Ramsay, pages 28, 31; Beken, 37, 41; N. Urvy, 33; Ben Hooper, 38; Josef Ciganovic, 107, 141, 149, 153; Patrick Gonat, 155, 156; The Spanish National Tourist Office, 13, 14, 18, 20, 62, 73, 102, 112, 121, 162, 174, 179.

I am grateful to Keith Blount for the specially drawn maps on pages 61, 81, 101, 119, 143, 161.

Contents

1 The Spanish Mediterranean Coast

With sixty harbours in its six hundred miles of
Mediterranean coastline and islands, Spain offers a wonderful
cruising area for the yachtsman. Since frequent sunshine, blue
translucent waters, winter warmth and real economy living are
assured, it is surprising that the harbours are not crowded.
Unlike the so-called fashionable harbours of the French Riviera
you can tie up in Spanish Harbours at any time for almost any
time (subject to the time limits mentioned later) with the
possible exceptions of the smart marinas of Barcelona and Arenys
de Mar. In addition to this, travel by Spanish bus and train is
cheap so that it is possible to explore a great deal of the country
from your floating hotel base.

The coastline of Spain is varied and mostly beautiful and the
best place from which to appreciate it fully is undoubtedly the
deck of a yacht.

The Spanish Mediterranean coast and islands are charted in
twenty-nine British Admiralty charts, in five Cartas Nauticas of
the Instituto Hidrografico de la Marina of Cadiz, and in three
(but not completely) Blondel la Rougery charts published by
Editions Maritime et d'Outre-Mer. Whichever you select you
simply must have, in addition, The Admiralty Mediterranean
Pilot, Volume 1, (No. 45); this describes the Spanish coast,
islands and off-lying dangers from Gibraltar UP to the French
frontier, (and much else besides).

In this book we decided to arrange the sequence DOWN the
Spanish coast since most yachtsmen arrive in the Mediterranean
at the 'Pyrenees end' of Spain, having come down the Rhône or
through the Canal du Midi, emerging at Sète or La Nouvelle.
In fact, in my book on the French Canals, (*Through the French
Canals*, Nautical Publishing Company), I mentioned that many

yachtsmen thought of them simply as a route to the
Mediterranean and I endeavoured to persuade those with limited
time to remain in the French waterways.

At a pinch you could say that I am a poacher turned
gamekeeper, for when I began cruising the first thing I did was to
rush straight through France to the Mediterranean. It was
because of our meetings with yachtsmen in odd harbours from
Malta to Marbella, (and in many islands in between), that we
discovered that few had discovered the inland waterways that
had brought them there; this included ourselves at that time, and
thus began our voyages of exploration to the sheltered inland
waterways of Europe.

The smart marinas of Barcelona . . .

We have always returned to the Mediterranean of course. For one thing, you cannot comfortably winter anywhere in the inland waterways of France, Belgium or Holland; for another . . . the Mediterranean beckons from time to time, and then it is tempting to come down the Rhône or along the Rhône-à-Sète Canal to spend a while pottering around harbours for a change.

There is no doubt that the Mediterranean exerts an almost irresistible influence upon the average yachtsman who dreams of the day when he will take his boat down through France, perhaps next year, perhaps on retirement; the special charm of the dream is that it is realisable.

When you buy a boat you buy some good quality dreams but most of them are bounded by reality. Pictures of yachts lying in glamorous-sounding harbours across the big seas excite envy, perhaps, but rarely ambition, for it seems that only a small minority of yachtsmen have the skill, endurance or desire to cross oceans.

Although the Mediterranean is a thousand miles from England, a special attraction is that the doorway leading to it is just there

. . . and Arenys.

across the Channel, almost within view and only hours away.

But there is no point in even considering a cruise down the Spanish coast unless you have time to spare, and the more time the better; in fact it needs the sort of time that normally comes to a man only on his retirement. Having said this it must be admitted that we have met many younger people on extended cruises in the European waterways and Mediterranean; couples, some with children, who have sold up everything to take an exciting year or two from dull routine.

Amongst extended cruising folk retired couples are naturally in the majority because they have the blessed gift of time. If any yachtsman doubts his physical ability, (or that of his wife), to manage such a trip at retirement age this doubt may be quickly dispelled. All over the Mediterranean and the inland waterways of Europe we have met retired couples, (two over eighty years of age), enjoying better health and better living in their boats than ever would be possible in the dreary retirement routine that most couples are condemned to at home.

Even if living onboard was to be more expensive than living ashore it would still be well worthwhile in terms of better health and a more lively interest in life. Yet in fact it is very much cheaper, and particularly is this so on the Spanish coast. The Spanish coast is ideal for boating 'potterers' like us, with plenty of harbours spaced at convenient distances apart. We have never had any enthusiasm for strenuous passage-making for we like to be snug in harbour every night. Indeed, the only justification for night sailing, to my mind, is to experience that good-to-be-alive moment when the dawn arrives and you seem to have the whole world to yourself.

The attractions of the Costa Brava and the Costa del Sol are well known to many holidaymakers; when you hear that twenty-five million visit Spain each year you imagine the whole coast to be a solid jam of people. Fortunately the package-deal merry-go-round circulates the multitudes from gleaming hotel to beach to souvenir shops to hotel to beach . . . and leaves the harbours alone.

Your flag will always attract fellow countrymen to your boat whatever harbour you are in; sometimes they have their uses as free-meal-and-bath tickets if you are in the mood.

The Costa Brava and the Costa del Sol are at each end of the Spanish Mediterranean coast and there are three Costas in between, plus the Balearic islands.

an Feliu de Guixols Club Nautico on the Costa Brava.

Costa Brava From the French frontier to Blanes the Catalan coast has been named the Costa Brava, (rugged or wild coast).

This coast is a stretch of rocky coves with pine forests running right down to the sea, and sandy beaches. Cape Creus will be seen as the focal point of this grandeur, with the Gulf of Rosas providing a contrast, followed by more headlands and bays to Blanes.

Port Bou, Port de la Selva, Cadaques, Rosas, Estartit, Palamos, San Feliu de Guixols, Tossa de Mar and Blanes are the harbours of the Costa Brava.

Open sandy beaches more than a mile long will be seen; looked at through the glasses you rejoice that the concentration of holidaymakers is here rather than in the comparative quiet and seclusion of the harbours.

The railway coming up from Barcelona can be seen following the coast to Blanes; it then goes inland to Gerona and Figueras, returns to the coast at Llansa and crosses into France at Port Bou. There are bus services to the main towns on this line from the coast and Gerona is linked to San Feliu de Guixols by railway.

Places of interest within easy reach of the Costa Brava are Gerona, Figueras, the ski resorts of La Molina and Nuria, the hot mineral spring spa, Caldas de Malavella, the monastery of Ripoll, and La Bisbal where attractive pottery is made in designs of fish and birds.

Costa Dorada Beyond Blanes a succession of wide, sandy beaches come into view and this coast of fine golden sand, extending as far as Cape Tortosa, is known as the Costa Dorada, (golden coast).

From Barcelona you will see that the beaches and rocky coastline alternate. From Sitges, past the harbours of Villanueva y Geltru and Tarragona, the beach extends as far as Cape Salou, next rocks appear, then another section of beach to the Ebro delta.

Harbours of the Costa Dorada are Arenys de Mar, Barcelona, Puerto de Garraf, Puerto de Vallcarca, Villenueva y Geltru, Tarragona, Puerto de Cambrils, Ametlla de Mar and Alfaques.

Barcelona and Tarragona are, of course, large commercial and industrial cities but the commerce and industry does not seem to intrude too much into the yacht harbours, except, perhaps, sometimes in Tarragona when the wind and a nearby factory

(left) Barcelona is in the centre of the Costa Dorada.

chimney conspire to lay a film of dust over the harbour.

The railway and the road can be picked out running the entire length of this coast. In addition to Barcelona and Tarragona, places of interest within easy reach are Montserrat, the monastery set in magnificent mountain scenery with the famous boys' choir, Igualada with its renaissance buildings, Montblanch, the old Catalan seat of Government encircled by walls and listed as a National Monument, Villafranca del Panades, the wine centre with its wine museum, 15th century wall and fine gates.

Costa Del Azahar From San Carlos de la Rapita, just beyond the Ebro delta, to Oliva is the Costa del Azahar, (orange blossom coast).

After the wide expanse of beach more rocky headlands and then more sand come into view, Vinaroz and Benicarlo being followed by the spectacular rock of Peniscola.

This is the chief orange and rice growing region with large areas of orchards. A reputation for the cultivation of carnations has also been established here.

From Vinaroz, across the Gulf of Valencia to Cape San Antonio, the view from the sea can be confusing for a series of lagoons have been created in the flat coastline. Duck shooting is popular here in October and November.

The harbours of the Costa del Azahar are San Carlos, Vinaroz, Benicarlo, Peniscola, Castellon, Burriana, Valencia, Cullera and Gandia.

Places of interest within easy reach are the Roman/Moorish town of Tortosa in a unique setting on the River Ebro, the attractive mountain town of Alcoy, Jativa with the castle of the Borgias, and Sagunto with its Roman theatre.

Costa Blanca From Playa de Vergel to the Cape de Gata, east of Almeria is the Costa Blanca, (the white coast).

After Cape San Antonio the rocks and bays return again and the beaches diminish in size. The major promontory is Cape de la Nao although the Penon Ifach, guarding the little fishing port of Calpe, looks more striking from the sea.

The bay of Benidorm that follows is of no interest to the yachtsman unless he is pining for rush-hour proximity with his vociferous compatriots in sweltering queues for Egg and Chips, Fish and Chips, English Tea, Cornish Pastie, English Bangers, or Red Barrel. Benidorm is the mecca of the package holiday maker but there is no yacht harbour there, the nearest being at Altea. The main item of interest in this area is the mountain village of Guadalest, to which the approach is hewn from rock.

After the beaches of the Murcia region and the harbours of Alicante and Santa Pola, are sandy stretches and lagoons, the largest of which is the Mar Menor, covering about sixty square miles and, from seawards, looking like an extension of the sea. There is, in fact, a small entrance between the sandspits. The Mar Menor will be seen to be a newly developing area; the water temperature in it is 10° higher than that of the Mediterranean, from which it is separated by a thin sandy strip.

The coast then becomes rocky again as far as Cape Gata; in this section is Cartagena, the Mediterranean naval base, easily distinguishable by the forts at each side of the narrow entrance.

Alicante and Murcia are garden areas of Spain producing dates, carnations, citrus fruits, almonds and vegetables.

You will see people bathing on this coast at almost any time of the year.

The harbours of the Costa Blanca are Denia, Javea, Calpe, Altea, Alicante, Santa Pola, Torrevieja, Portman, Cartagena, Mazarron, Aquilas, and Garrucha.

Nearby places of interest are Murcia with its strong Moorish aspect and Roman traces, Elche with its date palm forest, Lorca which has a 13th century castle and baroque buildings, Huercal Overa, a lace centre and the nearby caves of Almanzora.

Costa Del Sol   The Costa del Sol, (the sunny coast), runs from Cape de Gata, past Gibraltar to Tarifa Point.

From the sea this coast has a rugged outline relieved by sandy bays such as those at Almeria, Motril and Malaga. There are harbours here and also at Adra, Almunecar, Fuengirola, Torremolinos, the new Jose Banus marina and Esetepona.

Because the coast is so sheltered and so comparatively near to Africa it has justly earned its title as the Sunny Coast. If you do not care for heat you should avoid this area in the summer months; but if you fancy working on deck in shorts in January this is the place for you to winter. Adjoining the sherry region this coast has six golf courses and a good ski resort in the Sierra Nevada, 43 miles away, where the season is from November to June.

Places of interest within easy reach are the Sierra Nevada mountains and the ski resort of the same name, Granada, Alhama de Granada, Guadix, Antequera, picturesque Coin, the celebrated Nerja caves, Ronda with its three spectacular bridges, Tajo gorge and historic buildings and the Caves of Benaojan

nearby with prehistoric murals, stalactites etc.

Balearic Islands   The Balearic Islands lie 80 to 130 miles east of Spain. The most southerly islands, Ibiza and Formentera, are opposite Valencia; Majorca is almost opposite Barcelona, 123 miles away, while Minorca is the northernmost of the group.

Each island has its own character and different languages or dialects are spoken as well as Spanish.

Majorca's coastline is a succession of beaches and sheltered coves of fine sand, spread over 187 miles. Principal places of interest to yachtsmen are Palma, Andraitx, Soller, Pollensa, Alcudia, Cala Ratjada, Cala Figuera, Porto Colom, Porto Cristo and Porto Petro.

Of general interest are the limestone Drach Caves with the largest underground lakes in Europe and the Caves of Hams, Valldemosa with its fine Carthusian monastery where Chopin stayed, the 17th century monastery of Lluch, the picturesque Arta village and its caves.

Ibiza is distinguished by sparkling white, Moorish type houses against a background of splendid beaches. Ibiza seems to attract artists, many of whom have settled here; for the yachtsman there is Ibiza, San Antonio and Santa Eulalia.

Minorca attracts the least number of tourists but has fine beaches on its 124 miles of coasts. It was occupied by the British for nearly a hundred years around the 18th century and there are reminders of this. Of interest to yachtsmen are Ciudadela and more so Port Mahon, considered to be the best natural harbour in the Mediterranean and a favourite of Lord Nelson.

Of general interest is the megalithic monument of La Naveta de Tudons near Ciudadela, the Golden Farm where Nelson and Lady Hamilton lived. Admiral Collingwood's house, now a hotel, can be visited.

Formentera is 62 square miles in area; its only port is Cala Savina, three miles from the 'capital' of San Francisco Xavier.

On your map of Spain you will see rivers marked but they are not of much interest to the yachtsman; used for irrigation and hydro-electric power, not much of their water ever reaches the Mediterranean. River beds that can be seen by the coast are mostly dry, certainly in the summer droughts, and the rough homes, vegetation and cart tracks observed in the sun-baked mud

(*left*) Almeria has a pleasant harbour on the Costa de Sol.

Soller is an attractive summer harbour in Majorca, but in winter time squalls sometimes whistle down from the mountain.

of the river beds cause one to imagine that the presence of water there is unknown. Yet floods are likely from October to March and there have been disasters in the Ebro, Segura and Jucar. As recently as 1957 eighty people were drowned and extensive damage caused by the flooding of the River Turia.

Fishing Craft There are big fishing fleets all along the coastline and islands; in some harbours they are segregated, in others the yachtsman shares the quay wall with the fisherman. We have always found them to be kind, considerate and helpful even though there must have been many times when we have inconvenienced them.

Trying to clamber up high quay walls from our coach roof we are often yanked up by strong Spanish arms, the fishermen running from their nearby boats to help us.

Looking for a place to tie up in a fishing harbour we drift in the centre when the fishing boats are in, until we are noticed and a suitable place is indicated to us; then willing hands reach out for our warps and make us fast. If the necessity arises we have found that fishermen have appeared on our deck to help us. When first this happened we were trying to squeeze into a space that seemed scarcely long enough for us, but a wiry little fisherman had pointed it out to us and so we tried it. He secured the bow warp offered to him by my wife, leapt on deck, grabbed the stern warp, leapt ashore and secured it, leapt back onboard again to check that everything was secured inboard to his satisfaction, beamed with the pleasure of having been of service to us and was gone.

'You must give him something,' my wife urged.

I climbed up the quay and went along the lines of fishing boats in search of him. When I found him he beamed again until he suspected that I was going to offer him money. He refused indignantly with a pride comparable to that which drove Don Quixote on to his famous exploits. A cash tip is still considered something of an insult in the less 'enlightened' areas of Spain. A hearty handshake, a smile and thankyou is much more expected and appreciated.

Coming into Vinaroz some months ago the harbour was deserted so we tied up to the quay wall and went ashore. When we returned we could not see our boat for fishing boats that had come in in our absence and completely surrounded us. The fishermen thought it a big joke; although they were busy landing their catch they paused in their work to offer us some of it. Later we jumped up to the quay with our fuel cans. Although

'We could not see our boat for fishing craft.'

they were ready to go home, two of them walked with us to show us to the fuel pumps in the nearby town and then insisted on carrying them all the way back to the harbour for us. Since they do not sleep on board the fishing boats when in harbour we were left in peace for the night, but we were rocked awake when they left early next morning, after which we had the quay to ourselves again.

We speak no Spanish and few fishermen speak English but we smile and manage well enough with sign language.

Most of the fishing fleets work in daylight, bringing in their catches for the evening quay-side markets where many wait for their supper. The exceptions are the night fishing boats with the powerful acetylene lamps—the Lamparas—that attract fish to the side of the boat. Rocking at anchor over the black water, this is no job for anyone with a weak stomach and if you are invited to join such a trip, as you probably will be, you would be wise to excuse yourself.

A type of fishing activity for which the yachtsmen should be on the look-out, not only off the Spanish coast but elsewhere in the Mediterranean, is tunny fishing. The tunny nets are of such strength that if you had the misfortune to run into one you would have the greatest difficulty in getting out without propellor damage.

The fishing season varies slightly, but off the Spanish coast and islands it is usually from February to October. Each net is

'Where many wait for their supper.'

worked by two boats or buoys and they show by day a white flag with a black A in its centre, and by night two red lights disposed vertically on the seaward boat or buoy of the net. When engaged in dragnet fishing the boats exhibit a torchlight or flare on the side on which the net is hauled, in addition to the lights prescribed by the regulations.

When trawlers are fishing in pairs, to warn an approaching vessel not to pass between them, they show a flare on the same side as the trawl, in addition to the tricolour light and the white light prescribed. All the necessary guidance is set out on page 19 of your *Mediterranean Pilot, Volume* 1; as advised earlier you should have this onboard.

Tunny nets would be a menace if not taken into account but charts show the positions where these great nets are to be encountered so that precautions can be taken accordingly.

Pilotage   Lights along the coast are very good if you have to be out at night. Personally, and I think it worth repeating, I much prefer to be snug in harbour, and the Spanish harbours are so near to each other that there is no need to make night passages. Lifeboat stations and life-saving apparatus are not numerous.

It is not prudent to cruise too close along the coast for a better view of the country as there are offshore dangers, wrecks, rocks or the tunny nets already mentioned. About three miles off may be considered safe, or five when rounding headlands. Obviously you should never be too close to a lee shore, particularly in a sailing yacht; near inshore you sometimes experience contrary winds that blow one way one moment and the opposite way the next, and this could cause havoc to your gear that would be serious if you were too close to the land.

Spanish signal stations are distinctive, distinctive enough, that is, to be readily identifiable from the *Pilot*; many are like miniature castles, painted white or with white and black vertical stripes.

Cruising in Spain   Wherever you put in down the Spanish coast and islands you are quite likely to find another cruising boat, and most of them contain contented couples pottering economically from one sunny harbour to another; or sometimes remaining in harbour for weeks at a time luxuriating in a peaceful inertia. It is possible to do this in all Spanish harbours for as little as ten pesetas a day if a charge is made at all, although the marinas are obvious exceptions, offering one or two days free and then a rate in the region of a hundred pesetas a day.

You hear tales of assertive Spanish police but you can completely ignore such stories unless you are the sort of person who runs foul of the law in your own country. Generally the people who complain about anything are those who invite complaint.

Spanish Customs formalities are no different from those in any other country; you will not be bothered unless you provide a reason. But you will need to be patient, for officials in Spain are never in a hurry. Why not emulate them?

Whatever your views of the Spanish political situation it is surely wise to reflect that the Spanish people have had a tough time in your lifetime and mine; that they were completely ostracized by the United Nations until as recently as 1955 and were, in fact, almost bankrupt until the mutual defense and aid pact was signed with the United States.

Industrial recovery followed and tourism was encouraged at about the same time so that Spain is now host to around twenty-five million visitors a year. Fortunately few, if any, of these visitors have the slightest awareness of the difficulties Spain has overcome; unfortunately they are also equally unaware of the names of Lope de Vega, Cervantes or Goya.

The Spanish Mediterranean coast and islands offer you sunny harbours, sunny people, cheap living and a wealth of interest and exploration. Why not take a year off to cruise there before its potential is realised by the yachting crowd?

Having invited you to take a year off it should be mentioned that, officially, a boat may be kept in Spain for six months of each calendar year and then it should be sealed by the Customs or import duty paid. This is the official line; but all around you find people enjoying their second and third *year* in Spain. Some of them have taken the trouble to acquire a temporary import certificate but most have simply not bothered. If a yachtsman makes a nuisance of himself the 6-month rule is applied; otherwise, it seems, the authorities do not bother to enforce it.

2 Suitable and Unsuitable Boats

Most letters I receive seek information regarding the suitability, or otherwise, of various types of boat. For instance:—

'You do not mention the * * * * * class. Does this mean that it is not suitable for the French/Belgian etc., waters?'

Of course not. With over two hundred series production yachts in existence it would take a complete book to describe them all. I simply try to indicate certain types because they would be suitable, or to demonstrate a point, and mention of a particular class of yacht is the easiest way to provide a simple illustration. Omission is by no means a criticism; within the space available I try to mention as many classes as are necessary.

In using the word 'suitable' it is apparent that the consideration is not only the suitability of the craft for cruising the Spanish coast; but suitable for how many people? In our experience the average complement of long distance cruising boats is two.

To consider voyaging down the Spanish coast you need to think in terms of a three months cruise minimum, a long time for any amicable relationship to endure in the close confines of a yacht. Husband and wife partnerships endure the long term boating life not only because they have to but because the proximity seems to bring out the best and simplest values in the married relationship; and, of course, you have to be reasonably fond of each other to even consider embarking upon such an experience. The fact remains that the great majority of long distance boating couples we have met in our travels are really happy people; all aspects of life are shared and a much purer set of values seem to prevail than in life ashore.

From which you will conclude that I consider the term 'suitable' to mean suitable for two; and a boat with suitable accommodation for two, yet completely manageable by two would

not exceed 45ft. Reference to more than two berths simply
indicates availability of holiday or temporary accommodation for
relatives and friends; but do not entertain the thought of a long
term cruise with friends unless you possess the most saintly of
dispositions.

My previous yachting guide books have been about the
European inland waterways where a short holiday might be spent
in a craft possessing only limited comfort. Once you start thinking
about a cruise down the Spanish coast we have agreed that you
must obviously consider a trip of several months duration and
you will need a boat with as much living room as you can
afford.

To have to live and sleep in the same cabin gets tiresome after
a week or so and you would be well advised to try to get a boat
where the sleeping accommodation does not have to double up
for day living as well. An aft sleeping cabin is ideal, of course.

In considering suitable boats in these days of mass production
it is usual to think of class or series production boats. Except for
the millionaire species, the days of 'one-off' production is long
ago and far away; although it is an interesting fact that in the
period of change to mass production, motor-cruiser building has
continued along more individual lines than the building of sailing
yachts. In the latter case the necessary standard lay-out appears
to have been more widely acceptable; out of 160 production
sailing yachts that appeared in *Bristow's Book of Yachts* of eight
years ago, only 12 are being built today. There are also 12
production motor cruisers that have continued building throughout this period but from an original total of only sixty.

Aft cabins are most often found in motor cruisers; the after
part of the majority of sailing yachts is given over to a cockpit
in which to engage in the business of sailing. There are some
sailing yachts with after cabins, the best known, probably, being
the Hillyard family followed by the Fairey Atalantas.

Some years ago Hillyard's built a charming little 6-tonner with
an after cabin. I can remember tying up alongside one in
Portoferraio, Elba, and being amazed at the amount of
accommodation that had been squeezed into so small a boat.
You may remember that one of them, (*Ragged Robin*), featured
in Anthony Rushworth-Lund's book *By way of the Golden Isles*, the
story of a trip through the French Canals to the Balearic Islands.

The Hillyard 6-tonners are no longer built but they appear on
the second-hand market now and then at around £1500.

12-ton Hillyard.

The smallest Hillyard built recently is the 8-tonner but this version has an aft cockpit. The 9-tonners and 12-tonners have aft cabins and are ideal for extended cruising and living aboard.

The 9-ton Hillyard is 32ft LOA with a beam of 8ft 6in and a draft of 4ft 6in. There is full headroom in the main and after cabins.

The 12-ton Hillyards are 35ft LOA, beam 9ft 6in and draft

4ft 9in. They possess a great deal more living accommodation
than the majority of boats of similar size.

The Fairey Atalanta was designed in conjunction with Uffa
Fox and is unusual in that she has retractable bilge keels. LOA
is 26ft, beam 7ft 9in and draft 15in with the keels up and
5ft 9in with them lowered. With round moulded topsides the
Atalanta looks a bit like a submarine and certainly resembles
one below. Built of hot moulded marine ply the hull is claimed
to be resistant to marine borers and to be tougher than
conventional planked construction. With a sail area of 244 square
feet one would not expect the sailing performance to be
spectacular but it is adequate for the variable winds of the
Mediterranean. Second-hand Atalantas can be bought quite
inexpensively and are ideal for Mediterranean pottering, for the
inland waterway trip to get you there, and for extended living
aboard. There is also a 31ft Atalanta.

Having mentioned marine borers I should, perhaps, enlarge
upon the susceptibility of various types of hulls to the dreaded
teredo which, judging by some of the letters I receive, many
people imagine to be queuing up at the mouth of the Rhône,
ready to pounce.

Fibre-glass and steel hulls are impervious, of course, and similar
resistance is claimed for the hot moulded marine ply hulls
mentioned above. Teak is not a favourite meal of the teredo since
it is much too tough a wood; any other type of wooden hull
could be attacked if the under-water painting or anti-fouling
was neglected and if the boat was left, say, in stagnant water.
A boat that is regularly painted and regularly kept on the move
does not run much risk.

At one time I would have regarded this as a somewhat careless
over-simplification of the position. Years ago when I first
proposed visiting the Mediterranean I was somewhat appre-
hensive, foolishly listening to well-attired yachting gentlemen who
spoke of the perils of the teredo in the Mediterranean. The fact
that these gentlemen had been no nearer to the Mediterranean
than Yarmouth, Isle of Wight, did not deter me from seeking a
quotation for sheathing my hull; since the cost of doing so was
about a quarter the value of my boat I could not afford to have
it done.

Later, in a Spanish harbour, we visited a boatyard and, to my
astonishment, found them building big fishing boats of softwood.

'But the teredo?' I queried.

'Fishing boats are always on the move', I was told. 'And if boats are kept painted we never have any trouble.'

Most Hillyards are built of softwood but you see them all over the Mediterranean. It must be admitted that most of them are lived aboard permanently and thus should receive the regular painting that keeps marine borers at bay.

An ideal type of craft for exploring the Spanish coast is the motor-sailer, for most of them have accommodation built from one end of the boat to the other, sometimes completely enclosed with a centre wheelhouse, sometimes with an aft cabin and steering shelter over a centre cockpit.

The enclosed wheelhouse is the more comfortable arrangement for permanent living, particularly if you do not have a toilet at each end of the boat; also, it is a security advantage to have only one front door. (Not, I would hasten to add, that security is a problem on the Spanish coast for you can safely leave gear lying around on deck there that you would lock up on the Hamble River). An additional benefit is that heat is retained throughout the boat in cold weather.

The business of handling sheets is a little more complicated with an enclosed wheelhouse but you are not constantly tacking in a motor-sailer, in fact, if the weather allows, you hold a course for most of the day. Mediterranean weather is contrary, it is true, in fact within a quarter of an hour you can experience winds blowing from opposite directions. But motor-sailers invariably have their sail plan split up into ketch rig so that the handling is manageable by two people.

Open steering shelters provide greater facility in sail handling with the sheets led directly into the cockpit; thus a sloop rig would be acceptable with a shelter arrangement, a splendid example being the Salar.

Designed by Laurent Giles and Partners the Salar is 39ft LOA with a beam of 11ft 3in and a draft of 5ft 3in. This draft is rather on the deep side for coming through the canals to the Mediterranean, in fact it would preclude 'coming across the corner' from St. Malo to St. Nazaire for instance, though not through the main routes down—Le Havre, Paris, Lyons and the

(right) Salar.

Rhône. With a Perkins 4/236M diesel the Salar has a range of 1000 miles at a cruising speed of 7 knots. Salars provide excellent accommodation for up to six people and can be very comfortable.

A designer who has specialized in motor-sailers is Walter Rayner, best known, perhaps, for his Atlantic Class, 38ft LOA, beam 11ft 6in and draft 5ft. With provision for six berths in separate cabins this is an ideal boat for Mediterranean cruising and good value.

A smaller Rayner design is the Cape class, 33ft 4in LOA, 10ft beam and 4ft 8in draft. Similar in design to the Atlantic, but with five berths in two separate cabins, the Cape is an ideal boat for extended living onboard yet well within the management capabilities of husband and wife; the open shelter cockpit is appreciated when you find the Spanish sunshine and the various sheets are to hand without moving from the cockpit which is an asset.

Rayner's Lundy Class is an enclosed centre wheelhouse motor sailer, built on MFV lines with 37ft 3in LOA, beam 11ft and draft 4ft 6in. She has sleeping cabins at either end of the boat and a large deck saloon in the middle.

There are more motor-sailers designed with open centre cockpits than with enclosed; you will find that the former carry a greater sail area than the latter, from which it would seem to follow that ready access to the sheets is the design influence. Thus, it would probably be a reasonably accurate generalisation to say that open cockpit motor-sailers have a better sailing performance than enclosed cockpit motor-sailers.

But, to my mind, sailing performance should not be the primary consideration when choosing a boat for extended Mediterranean cruising, where most passage making is done with assistance from the engine. It cannot be repeated too often that sailing in the Mediterranean can be a very frustrating business, although I accept that nobody believes this until they try. If it was true, and it well might be, that every one ounce of sailing performance took away one inch of comfort, I would strongly advise going for comfort every time in choosing a boat to live aboard for any length of time.

(right) Cape.

Since motor-sailers with all enclosed accommodation are in the minority, the Sole Bay is of interest. Built on pilot boat lines she is 35ft LOA with a beam of 10ft and a draft of 4ft 9in. The large, enclosed deck saloon gives plenty of protection from mistrals, tremontanas and other undesirable weather conditions and the rest of the accommodation is spacious. There is a 40ft version with more space and speed and these sometimes come on the second-hand market.

From the board of the same designer, Francis Jones, is the Inchcape, available in 32ft, 38ft and 45ft versions and built on the lines of the traditional Scottish seine net fishing boats. The Inchcape is a real little ship with solid bulwarks and decks; on the Spanish coast she might easily be mistaken for one of the fishing fleet returning home.

Sole Bay.

Another well known enclosed wheelhouse motor sailer is the Spey Class, also built heavily like a Scottish fishing vessel. The Spey 35 is 35ft LOA, beam 11ft 3in and draft 5ft, with six berths, an attractive galley and wheelhouse/dining saloon she is available with sloop or ketch rig.

The larger Spey is 40ft LOA with a beam of 12ft 6in and a draft of 5ft. With accommodation for up to eight the Spey 40 is easily handled under sail or power. You see Speys quite often in

Spey 40.

the Mediterranean; they are undoubtedly luxurious craft for permanent living.

Motor cruisers have more accommodation per given LOA than sailing craft because they do not have to be concerned with the business of sail stowage and sailing; the bigger engine space needed in a motor cruiser is invariably tucked away under the wheelhouse. There are not so many class or series production motor cruisers as there are sailing yachts; there are many more motor-boats of the day cruiser or run-a-bout type, of course, but we are only concerned here with craft possessing comfortable living accommodation.

My favourite at present is the displacement type of centre wheelhouse motor cruiser.

'May I enquire what sort of boat you have?' many readers enquire in their letters. Whilst I am happy to divulge this information I still think that choosing a boat is as personal a matter as choosing a wife and you will know as well as I do that many of them get more love and attention, (the boats I mean). Having owned five sailing boats we have now been converted to converting a TSDY for permanent living, taking out the two forepeak berths and installing a bathroom there. Our boat is 37ft LOA with a beam of 10ft and a draft of 3ft 6in. We have a large galley area in the living room, a centre wheelhouse from which we can comfortably watch the world go by, and a permanent bedroom aft. With side decks all round bordered by a beautiful mahogany rail we feel secure; the spacious foredeck is our sun lounging area. The twin screws are tucked well up in the hull form so that they are not the lowest part of the boat if we have the misfortune to touch bottom which, of course, we do from time to time, (and who does not?).

But, as I say, boats are personal; if you had my boat you would be sure to alter something and if I had your boat I would do the same. In discussing various types of boats in this chapter I accept that all we are doing is to generate ideas which may help you to find what is ideal for you.

There are a number of centre wheelhouse cruisers of no particular class on the second-hand market; there are also a great many people after them. The basic layout of a cabin on either side of the wheelhouse is the same in each but variations in the positioning of galley, toilet, bunks etc., seem to be limitless. Even with class motor cruisers, externally similar, the internal layout may not be the same.

Rampart.

A desirable standard cruiser is the Rampart, with a usual layout of fore cabin, stateroom, toilet compartment, wheelhouse, full width galley, saloon and aft cockpit. There are a number of Ramparts available on the second-hand market.

Demand for lower priced craft of this type has increased very much in recent years, which has helped to put the prices up. Even motor cruisers thirty or forty years old have asking prices of four or five times their building price when new. Unless you are a real handyman you should certainly not consider anything in need of renovation or repair; you can be quite certain that there is always a great deal more needing attention behind the obvious items which are often the easiest.

If you have plenty of money, of course, there is no problem; something like a Beecham 40 would be available to you. 40ft overall with a beam of 12ft 3in and a draft of 4ft, this displacement TSDY is constructed to a very high standard. With spacious accommodation for 5 or 6 persons, two toilet compartments, shower and galley better than many homes, (refrigerator, cooker with eye-level grill, automatic hot and cold water supply

Beecham 40.

throughout), the Beecham 40 is a boat to tempt you to sell up
your home and depart for the sunshine of the Spanish coast right
away.

Another luxury displacement cruiser in the 36ft type is the
Grand Banks; there are also 32ft, 42ft, 50ft and 57ft versions
available. With a hard chine and full length keel a smooth ride
is obtained. The big living room/wheelhouse is ideal for
Mediterranean living; the galley is in the same area, a nice
point since when you stop you often prepare meals and entertain
at the same time. The owner's stateroom has its own toilet and
shower. The distinctive flying bridge of the Grand Banks is a
splendid balcony from which to watch the Spanish coast drift
by, but it is quite a problem if a trip to the Mediterranean
through the French canals is contemplated, as the flying bridge
is too high out of the water to pass under a number of fixed
bridges. With a range of over 1000 miles at economic cruising
speed the Grand Banks is able to go 'round the corner' in convenient hops but not many motor-cruiser owners fancy this.

You can sneak across to Le Havre during a lull in a bad weather period and you are on the way to the Mediterranean; but you cannot attempt a Biscay crossing without the sanction of the weather man. The Grand Banks is ideal for the Mediterranean, therefore, but you would have to think about the problem of getting it there. The same applies to any flying bridge cruiser. Make sure that the height above the waterline is within the limits of the waterways you propose using, (or that the flying bridge is easily detachable, like the wheelhouses of the European barges).

My opinion is that most husband and wife crews could easily manage a cruiser across to Le Havre, down through France and down the Spanish coast—but the same couple should certainly not attempt the open sea passage to the Mediterranean unless they have considerable sea going experience.

You see many planing type cruisers in the smarter harbours of the Mediterranean; the Fairey Huntsman illustrated is typical. It is splendid to be able to go from place to place at forty knots if you fancy that sort of thing. But speed is expensive in terms of fuel, insurance, engine wear . . . and body-wear too, I should imagine. A boat for me is a place of peace, escape from tension,

Fairey Huntsman.

refreshment of the soul and that sort of thing into which engines should not intrude more than necessary. There would be precious little refreshment of my soul in the company of a 40-knot screaming diesel. These craft are intended as day cruisers, of course, and not for permanent living.

The type of motor cruiser most often seen in the Mediterranean is the open after cockpit variety with a saloon, galley, toilet and fore-peak berths. The Chris-Craft 31 Commander illustrated is a typical example but there are many variations in quality, accommodation lay-out and power units. You do not often find that this type of boat is chosen for permanent living, however.

What sort of boats do others choose in which to live for longish periods whilst exploring the Spanish coast and Mediterranean? For the most part, not very expensive ones, I am sorry to say. We creep in, like poor relations, to the glamorous marinas of Arenys and Barcelona and watch uniformed servants scrape from luxury rails alongside better varnish than our best. The main difference between us and all this luxury is that we appear to be happier, but then, we have escaped whilst the luxury is chained to the luxury-producing treadmill; his boat is a virtually unused symbol, ours is our life.

We met a contented couple in a Troll class in Tarragona.

Chris-Craft 31.

They had been cruising for a year and were thinking of buying a bigger boat in which to continue the life permanently. We gathered that they had not embarked upon the cruising life until retirement age.

Troll.

In Peniscola we came across another retired couple in a 40ft motor-sailer. We first saw them, wandering hand in hand, like a couple of contented water gypsies, laden with beautiful Spanish oranges and fresh vegetables from a nearby market. They were sun-tanned in March, fairly poor but completely happy.

A twin-screw diesel cruiser was the choice of a couple we met in Almeria; no less than four centre wheelhouse cruisers were flying the British flag when we entered Javea recently. To try to recall the different yachts that we have encountered in the Balearics is to blur the memory; at any time of the year the British flag, and many another foreign flag are everywhere in the islands.

Our common denominator seems to be a special aura of contentment. We have escaped.

We sit on sunny decks and drink our Spanish wine, (5p a bottle), and care not at all for tomorrow. Subject to the suggestions made in this chapter the best boat for you is the best that you can afford; the most important consideration for you is not the boat itself but your making of the decision to become a yachting gypsy. So sell all your possessions now and escape to the Mediterranean boating life; on the Spanish coast you will never regret it.

3 Equipment

To get to the Spanish coast it is likely that you will go
through the French canals, and the equipment needed for the
inland waterway journey is set out in *Through The French Canals*,
(Nautical Publishing Company).

Briefly, these items are:—

A dinghy that will stow inboard out of the way.

At least four 15 fathom $1\frac{1}{2}$in to 2in warps.

Necessary flags.

Adequate fenders; a minimum of four, large sausage shape.

Motor tyres, one for each 4ft of waterline; you will, of course,
dispose of these on arrival in the Mediterranean.

A plank for hanging outside of the tyres when alongside piles,
also to double up as a gangplank.

A ladder.

Boathooks and a pole for fending off in descending, sloping
sided locks.

A searchlight.

A hooter or syren.

Torches.

Planned-in-advance stowage on deck for masts, where
applicable.

Having come down through France the business of stepping
and preparing for sea will be done in a French port.

Some restowing will be necessary after the comparatively
smooth inland waterways. Be careful not to stow tins near to the
compass which will now be brought into use again; it is easily
done when store cupboards are sited on bulkheads the other side
of which might be the compass, only inches away. Take some
test bearings before you set off down the Spanish coast. Because
you may propose to 'hedge hop' and the disposition of Spanish

**Naviga-
tional** harbours is ideal for this, do not relax on your navigational duties for you can sometimes be shrouded in misty patches of fog without warning and you should know your position at any time.

An item of equipment that seems to be moving from the luxury into the essential category is an auto-pilot and it is claimed that they steer a better compass course than you or I. Particularly with a small crew it is a blessing to be able to escape from the tyranny of wheel or tiller; but do not let your ghost helmsman tempt you into relaxing your vigilance.

The little hand-bearing compass that we use is the one marketed by Offshore Instruments. Lit by beta radiation it magnifies bearings ten times which I find especially useful since I can read them without the aid of my glasses that always disappear when most wanted.

You will be equipped with a suitable RDF set and a nautical almanac giving the Mediterranean radio beacons; in fact your normal items of navigational equipment will be normal for the Spanish coast too, including the requisite charts of course.

The equipment needed for your boat is not so much specifically related to the requirements of a Spanish cruise as to the requirements of living onboard for the length of time that such a cruise entails. Obviously these requirements should all be attended to before you leave your home port.

Lockers Adequate stowage is the first essential. You cannot have too many cupboards and lockers; the ready-made cupboards that you buy in department stores are obviously much cheaper than those specially made for you by a boatyard. Take the precaution of measuring the dimensions of your doors and hatches first, though, for cupboards that look small in a store seem to transform into giant size when you try to manoeuvre them below decks.

Fuel and water capacity can often be increased by installing new tanks in out-of-the-way corners and the rubber variety are well suited for using up what would otherwise be unusable vacant space. Two people need at least a hundred gallons of water for convenient living on the Spanish coast where supply points are not always readily available in the harbours. It is a wise precaution to carry some 5-gallon containers to meet emergencies.

The water supply will be brought to your taps either by a manual or an electric pump; if electric you should carry a spare pump and the knowledge to fit it. Of course you will need to ensure that there is always a sufficiency of battery power to work it.

When you contemplate living onboard for a long time it is well worthwhile to find out as much as you can about 'the works' of everything onboard. Apart from the financial advantages of this, he is a happier man who can turn his hand to anything and is independent of others.

Ashore you take for granted the turning of a tap, the press of a switch; living afloat nothing can be taken for granted and this gives the life its interest and charm. Your creative talents will prefer the challenge of maintaining your little ship in preference to rotting before a television screen ashore.

Bottled Gas   In previous books I have expressed doubts about the wisdom of using bottled gas for cooking or heating, and I still feel that I would be somewhat diffident about using it in a boat with a petrol engine. But now I have diesel engines and I have received such assurances from the bottled gas experts that I have been happy to modify my views. If it is properly installed, properly used and regularly tested, (at least once a year), it is claimed that it is safe and particularly so when in company with a diesel engine.

As the Calor gas people say, it is a perfectly safe and reliable fuel but, like the gas you use at home, it needs to be handled with common sense.

Some appliances, such as the refrigerator and water heater, have a pilot light; you would imagine it to be obvious that these naked flames should be turned off before filling the boat with petrol fumes, when fuelling a petrol engine.

Any fuel uses up fresh air so that every compartment of your boat in which a gas appliance is situated should be properly ventilated. Usually all such compartments are, of course, but I recently went onboard a new luxury cruiser in which a water heater had been installed in a very small toilet compartment without any ventilation.

If builders of £50 000 yachts make these mistakes how, you might ask, are we ordinary mortals to know whether we have a safe installation or not? The answer is that the Calor people are pleased to tell you. They are extending their advisory service and you can call upon their experts at any time for free advice.

As an added precaution you can fit a gas detector which sounds an alarm if gas is escaping. Should this happen you put out all naked lights and turn off the gas at the cylinder.

And what, many people ask, should you do if there is a leak of gas into the bilges? The answer is that you get plastic buckets

or any similar container and 'scoop' the gas out over the side;
however much of an idiot you may feel to be rushing out into
the cockpit with buckets of nothing, this is what you have to do.
Perhaps it might make more sense to you if you tried a little
experiment; using a gas cigarette lighter, 'squirt' some gas into a
cup, then pour this 'nothing' into another cup and you will find
that you will be able to light it.

Coupled with these assurances we have received, there is
another reason that has caused us to change our minds and this
is the benefit of having an oven; living onboard permanently,
your menu needs greater variety than two-burner cookery can
provide.

Water Heating   A gas water heater, usually mounted over the sink, can supply
a number of outlets in addition to the sink tap, say at wash
basins or at a bath; but to enjoy this facility you must have a
pressurised water system, in other words an electric pump.

We took out the berths from our fore-peak and installed a small
bathroom there. The small bath we bought from a caravan
supplier. We could have had a shower unit fitted but it seemed
that it might require more water than a bath, also the disposal
of the waste water was more of a problem in our boat. We did
not want soapy water in the bilges. We moved the toilet to the
bathroom, taking it from what was quite a cramped space for
that purpose and converting the space to a generous work top
and stowage extension.

Refrigerator   Living in the Mediterranean you must have a refrigerator and
the bottled gas type is most impressive, but to operate it needs
the gas permanently on, and the same is so of the pilot light on
the water heater. I am assured that there is no danger provided
that one's equipment is regularly checked. Safeguards provide
that if either of these flames should be blown out by a draught,
the supply of gas would be automatically cut off.

Calor gas cylinders are not obtainable abroad but similar
supplies are available under different brand names. You should
take with you a Camping Gaz Connecting Tap No. 13/782 which
enables a Camping Gaz 907 cylinder to be connected up to your
Calor system.

Electric Power   Being your own water company, electricity board and gas
company all sounds a trifle intimidating when you set out to live
semi-permanently on a boat. If you allow your bottled gas to run
out you have no cooking nor hot water; if you allow your
batteries to run down you have no engine starting, no water

pump and therefore no water, neither H nor C, (except for your containers). Using your engine frequently, as you will when going from one Spanish port to another, it is likely that your batteries will stay sufficiently charged. You will probably know that if you fitted an alternator it would guarantee that your batteries would be fully charged with only about twenty minutes of running a day, but obviously this depends upon electricity used.

Many boats have generators to charge batteries. Some of the new 4-stroke petrol engines are quiet in operation, efficient and economical; make sure that you get one with a good charging rate and do not buy an AC/DC model if you only want the DC. Since a petrol generator entails carrying a supply of petrol onboard you should first check whether or not this invalidates your insurance cover if, apart from this, you are a 'diesel boat'.

Diesel generators are more expensive, noisier and heavier but often give a greater output and run no risk of offending your insurer.

With a generator onboard you can never be completely 'stuck' for electric power. With an alternator you could be if your batteries were too low to start the engine to work the alternator to charge the batteries.

With twin engines that each take starter power from separate batteries it is wise to carry a set of jumper leads so that an engine that will not start from its own battery can be started from an engine that will.

It all needs planning in advance. These major contributions to your basic comforts should be adequate, efficient, understood and backed up with key spare parts before you set off. When you see the splendid shops in Barcelona, Tarragona, Alicante, or Malaga, the well stocked chandleries and the gleaming yachts, (obviously serviced), you may wonder at the need for all this caution; but it is best to be prepared.

Fans   One item that you may well appreciate in the heat is an electric fan, and you can buy quite small and efficient models at most chandlers.

If you do run into any sort of trouble for which you have no remedy onboard you will find skilled Spanish help willingly and inexpensively available. In one of our earlier boats we were rounding Cape Creus on a hot, windless day when the needle of the engine temperature gauge announced a warning. On investigation we found that cooling water was escaping from what

Repairs appeared to be a hole in the block. We worked away at the bilge pump for a time and the engine cooled down; we started it up again and gingerly crept round to Rosas, a minor holiday resort.

Going ashore we found a small engine repair shop. They spoke no English and we speak no Spanish, but after a sign language dialogue we emerged with tins of Cemento Metalico, powder and liquid to be mixed. We worked away at mending the hole and, next day, took the tins back. Our new friends came down to the boat with us to make sure that all was well and refused to take more than twenty pesetas for their help.

I had noticed on the label that Cemento Metalico was made in Tarragona. When we arrived there I bought some tins of my own and I have them still, having transferred them from boat to boat. Their presence is an assurance that never again will I get a hole in my engine; in some mysterious way this is what spare parts are for.

Varnish vanishes in the Mediterranean heat; it blisters, dulls, and curls up. Exposed boards warp and refuse to fit if not continuously washed down. If you have a favourite brand of varnish or paint it will be handy to have supplies onboard. If you are re-varnishing and re-painting in preparation for your trip it would be wise to have more white painted areas than varnished.

Awnings Awnings and the necessary frames would be well worth considering if you can devise such protection for your 'sun deck' areas. Folding deck chairs or sun beds are no cheaper in Spain and should be taken with you.

The plank mentioned earlier will do duty as a stern gangway if necessary but you do not have to do as much stern-to-ing in Spanish harbours as you do in French. In most Spanish harbours you lie alongside the quay walls; in some of the marinas uniformed servants take your bow warp, direct you to your pontoon mooring and issue you with a copy of the club rules.

You will find a ladder useful, both for climbing back onboard after swimming and for scaling quay walls too high to climb.

Fire Extin- Lastly, but most important, fire extinguishers are so in-
guishers expensive in relation to the protection they provide that you would be foolish to economise on them.

4 Cost of Living

When you want some Spanish money you will need to look for the word *cambio*, (change).

You can live very inexpensively in Spain. If you were content to have most of your meals onboard and you did not object to a diet of fruit, vegetables, eggs, fish and wine you could live very cheaply indeed.

Practically everywhere you come ashore you will find a vegetable market with a display of produce that looks fresh because it really is. In many places there is a municipal market, a sort of food hall where the different stall-holders set out their colourful arrangements.

If you like olives you will be happy because Spain is the biggest producer of them in the world. Oranges are also plentiful and cheap as one would expect from one of the world's largest producers. Apricots and peaches, potatoes, greens, tomatoes, onions, almonds, artichokes are available everywhere in markets big and small. Experiencing higher average temperatures you find yourself living quite largely on salads and almost certainly feeling worthwhile benefit to your health, quite apart from the benefit to your pocket of course.

Groceries, as we understand them, are available everywhere in stores big and small, including Spar supermarkets. With self-selection language is obviously no problem. In most of the British community areas you will find many familiar tinned foods in the shops.

The meat situation in Spain has improved enormously in recent years and even a number of the smaller supermarkets now have a meat counter. For some odd reason butcher's shops seem to be hard to find. Many a time we have gone ashore with our shopping bag and found, without the slightest difficulty, the wine shop (naturally), the grocery shop, the bread shop (by getting a good fix on bread carrying citizens), but the location of the butcher has invariably required direction. Do not assume because you do not see a butcher's shop that one is not in the vicinity.

It is still a wise precaution to take some tins of minced steak with you; you can load quite a number in the bilges and they are a useful standby in emergencies.

Most of the poultry available looks somewhat emaciated; it seems that the chickens in Spain are kept as egg producers and that table bird production as we know it is unknown.

But there is a lot of protein in sardines and beautiful, plump large ones can be bought for the equivalent of a few pence at the evening fish auctions. All sorts of succulent fish are available from the fishing boats at practically every harbour you visit including sardines, anchovies, tunny, octopus, squid, cuttlefish, sea trout, eels, lobsters, crabs, cockles, mussels, crayfish, shrimps and king-sized prawns.

Eating Ashore   If you can afford to eat ashore you will find that Spanish restaurants are officially classified by the Government; standard fixed price menus are available according to classification. If you are in doubt about the wine list the un-bottled wine of the house, (*vino de la casa*), is likely to be the best value.

Perhaps the best known Spanish dish is *paella*, supposed to be at its best in Valencia so that you should certainly plan a meal ashore when you tie up at the hospitable yacht club there. The basis of *paella* is saffron flavoured rice into which is mixed prawns, pieces of fish, clams, pieces of meat and chicken and the result is served in the pan in which it is cooked, decorated with colourful pimento and green peas.

The Spanish dinner hour is much later than ours; if you do not go ashore until 10 pm you will still be welcome.

In the hot weather you will appreciate *gazpacho* which is ice cold soup covered with a veritable garden of chopped vegetables, sometimes including garlic and breadcrumbs.

Spanish cooking is often wrongly blamed for what is known as Spanish tummy but I think that a more probable reason for this is over indulgence in sunshine and wine. It is such a temptation to seek for our sun-starved bodies the beautiful Spanish sunshine; to work or lie about on deck practically in the nude is a great temptation at first because it is difficult for us to accept that the sun will be there again tomorrow.

Take with you your favourite sunburn preventatives and cures; in fact take with you a proper medicine chest, (you can buy them at most chandlers and they can be screwed to a toilet bulkhead out of the way), and fill it with your favourite remedies. There are chemists in Spain, of course, but they may not stock the particular remedy that you prefer.

And whilst on, or at least near, to this subject, you may wish to take a supply of toilet paper that you and your toilet favour. You will know that marine toilets can be fussy on this subject but they will not object to the toilet paper that you buy in Spain because it is not soft; you may object however.

Tissues cost more in Spain than in England. If you are a big user you will economise by taking a supply.

Spanish Wines Spanish wines do not enjoy the reputation of French wines, but it is obviously ridiculous of the wine snobs to claim that every French wine is superior to every Spanish. There are many French wines that I dislike and many Spanish wines that I like; the reverse is also true. Whether in France or in Spain you need to experiment to discover wines to your liking; in Spain this is a pleasant and inexpensive exercise.

Vino corriente is the local wine that you buy in the *bodegas* really quite cheaply, taking your own bottle to be filled from the huge barrels. You have the choice of *vino blanco*, (white), *vino tinto*, (red), or *vino rosado*, (rosé) with further variations of *seco*, (dry), *dulce*, (sweet) or *medio seco* (medium).

You can also buy liqueurs very cheaply on draught at many *bodegas*. Be careful to distinguish the contents of the bottles when you stow them back onboard; if you have filled a lemonade bottle with Cointreau or a Coca-Cola bottle with Benedictine and someone takes a good swig on a hot day you are going to have a candidate for the Commander's Report next morning. The French-named liqueurs that you buy, either on draught or in their familiar shaped bottles, are made in Spain under licence and are very much cheaper than the prices you are accustomed to pay for liqueurs. You can fairly easily persuade yourself that they are what they are supposed to be . . . unless you try the original.

A lovely Spanish drink to entertain or relax onboard with is *sangria*. You can make quantities of it inexpensively with red wine, a little brandy to taste, water, slices of orange, lemon and any other fruit you fancy, ice, sugar and soda.

You can buy your favourite gin at about a quarter of its cost to you at home and Spanish gin much cheaper still. Whisky is normally less expensive than in the UK; if this is your favourite drink you should stock up with a duty-free bonded store before leaving home, assuming that you qualify.

There are a number of Spanish brandies and perhaps you may find that the cheapest brands take your breath away at first but then, so do the prices.

As you would imagine there are all sorts of varieties of sherry in Spain, this being the characteristic Spanish drink; the various basic groupings are *finos* (pale and dry), *amontillados* (medium dry), and *olorossos* (dark, sweet, heavy, rich).

Beer is widely available either as keg beer (*cerveza de barril*) or bottled beer (*cerveza*).

Fresh Water　　Whilst on the subject of drinking perhaps I should mention water. We have always filled our tanks as opportunity offered, in harbours large and small, and have suffered no ill effects so far. If you are particularly fussy about this you can buy bottled water everywhere, the Vichy Catalan resembling French Vichy.

You can also buy milk everywhere. For the days when we may be too lazy to go ashore we usually carry a supply of Longlife milk cartons in the bilges. We also have tins of powdered milk onboard for emergencies. Another staple item of diet, bread, is not likely to tempt you much in Spain, but consider how good that will be for your waistline.

You will find in the markets a great variety of inexpensive cheeses that will tempt you and a greater variety of sausages that

An open air restaurant may be only a step away as in the marina at Puerto Jose Banus.

English-Spanish Shopping Vocabulary

anchovies—*anchoas*
apple—*manzana*
apricot—*albaricoque*
artichoke—*alcachofa*
asparagus—*espárrago*
bacon—*tocino*
banana—*plátano*
beans—*judias*
beef—*carne de vaca*
beefsteak—*bistec*
　　well done—*bien hecho*
　　rare—*poco hecho*
beer—*cerveza*
beetroot—*remplacha*
biscuits—*galletas*
bottle opener—
　　abrebotellas
bread white—*pan blanco*
bread brown—*pan negro*
Brussels sprouts—*coles*
　　de Bruselas
butcher—*carnicero*
butter—*mantequilla*
cabbage—*col*
cake—*pastel*
carrot—*zanahoria*
cauliflower—*coliflor*
celery—*apio*
cheese—*queso*
chemist—*farmacéutico*
cherries—*cerezas*
chicken—*pollo*
chocolate—*chocolate*
chops—*chuletas*
cod—*bacalao*
coffee white—*cafe con*
　　leche
coffee black—*cafe solo*
crab—*cangrejo*
crayfish—*cangrejo de rio*
cream—*nata*
cucumber—*pepino*

dates—*dátiles*
duck—*pato*
eels—*anguilas*
eggs—*huevos*
figs—*higos*
fish—*pescado*
fishmonger—*pescadero*
fruit—*fruta*
garlic—*ajo*
grape—*uva*
grapefruit—*pomelo*
grocer—*abacero*
haddock—*róbalo*
ham—*jamón*
herrings—*arenques*
honey—*miel*
hors d'oeuvres—
　　entremeses
ice—*hielo*
ice-cream—*helado*
jam—*dulce*
kidney—*riñon*
lamb—*cordero*
lemon—*limón*
lettuce—*lechuga*
liver—*higado*
lobster—*langosta*
mackerel—*caballa*
marmalade—*mermelada*
marrow—*calabacin*
meat—*carne*
melon—*melón*
milk—*leche*
mushroom—*seta*
mussels—*moluscos*
mustard—*mostaza*
mutton—*carnero*
olives—*aceitunas*
olive oil—*aceite de oliva*
omelette—*tortilla*
onion—*cebolla*
oranges—*naranjas*
oyster—*ostra*

pastry—*pasteles*
peach—*melocotón*
pear—*pera*
peas—*guisantes*
pineapple—*piña*
plaice—*gallo*
plum—*ciruela*
pork—*carne de cerdo*
potato—*patata*
prawns—*gambas*
prunes—*ciruela pasa*
rabbit—*conejo*
raisins—*pasas*
raspberry—*frambuesa*
rice—*arroz*
salad—*ensalada*
salmon—*salmón*
salt—*sal*
sardine—*sardina*
sausages, beef—*salchicha*
　　de buey
sausages, pork—*salchicha*
　　de cerdo
shrimp—*quisquilla*
sirloin steak—*solomillo*
snails—*caracoles*
sole—*lenguado*
soup, clear—*consommé*
soup, thick—*sopa*
spinach—*espinaca*
stew—*estofada*
strawberry—*fresa*
sugar—*azúcar*
sweetbreads—*criadillas*
tea—*té*
tin opener—*abrelatas*
toast—*tostada*
tomato—*tomate*
trout—*trucha*
tuna—*atún*
veal—*ternera*
vinegar—*vinagre*
water—*agua*

will not. Lady members of the crew should stay onboard at tea time for this is the hour when the pastryshops beckon to the detriment of the Spanish ladies waistlines.

Fuel   The fuel industry in Spain is a Government monopoly controlled by Campsa. Fuel is not always conveniently available in the harbours so that you would be wise to top up your tanks wherever and whenever you can. Branded motor oils are available but there is no guarantee of getting your favourite brand; if you can stow a few drums in your engine compartment it would be a sensible precaution.

Despite the resourcefulness of Spanish mechanics you would be well advised to take with you a kit of engine spares, also electric light bulbs of the necessary power and fitting. In many harbours there are ship and yacht building and repair yards if you need help in the marine department.

Harbour dues may amount to ten or fifteen pesetas a day, if they are charged at all; in many harbours there does not seem to be anybody around to levy a charge. In the marinas the initial stay, varying from twenty-four to seventy-two hours, is free and then a fairly high marina tariff comes into operation. You are handed details on arrival so that you have time to consider whether you will not pay or stay.

5 Weather—and Miscellaneous Items

The tourist season is generally regarded as extending from April to October because most people take their holidays to coincide with the better weather expected then. On the Spanish coast there is no such seasonal limitation upon the yachtsman who can move to sunshine somewhere at any time of the year; at the height of summer there will be a temptation to move *from* the sunshine, when the heat is almost unbearable and the varnish peels almost before your stupefied eyes.

In many places the travel firms are now organising what they term winter seasons, and well they might for the sun is always somewhere on the Spanish coast.

For the yachtsman 'weather' means a little more than sunshine, and even if only short hops from harbour to harbour might be contemplated it is as well to avoid being caught out if you can avoid it; not that Mediterranean weather is always predictable but there are signs, such as the unusual clarity of the atmosphere that precedes a north-westerly mistral, or the cumulo-nimbus cloud banking that shuts out the horizon and heralds the levanter.

Winds arrive in the Mediterranean through gaps in mountain ranges. The north-westerly wind down the Rhône valley is best known as the *mistral*, or *el maestral* or *tramontana* on the Spanish coast. This increases in strength away from the land.

The fishing boats are the best barometers to watch for impending gales or for the ending of gales; if they do not go out because of weather, neither should you.

It is said that if the *mistral* has not arrived by 10.00 in summer, (noon in winter), then it is not coming that day. When it does come it may last for two hours or two weeks, but two days would be a nearer average duration.

Winds   Local winds or eddies are sometimes experienced if you are too close in to a steep shore. Winds known as *contrastes* can blow from opposite directions almost, it seems, within minutes of each other; blowing towards a steep shore they meet winds descending towards them and the result is a sudden blast arriving, apparently, from nowhere.

As you would expect, you get most *mistrals* in the winter and near the Gulf of Lions; in spring and autumn they occur less frequently and in summer hardly at all.

Spanish storm signals are as follows:—

GALE FROM NW—MISTRAL
by day   ..   ..   a cone, point upwards
by night   ..   ..   2 red lights, vertically
GALE FROM NE—LEVANTER
by day   ..   ..   2 cones, points upwards, vertically
by night   ..   ..   a red light over a white light
GALE FROM SE
by day   ..   ..   a cone pointing downwards
by night   ..   ..   2 white lights, vertically
GALE FROM SW
by day   ..   ..   2 cones pointing downwards
by night   ..   ..   a white light over a red light

A square shape displayed by day or a red light between two white lights, vertically means a local gale, all boat movement suspended.

by day   ..   ..   2 cones points together
by night   ..   ..   a white light over 2 red lights
means a gale of moderate force; harbour closed to small craft.

by day   ..   ..   2 cones bases together
by night   ..   ..   3 red lights, vertically
means a severe gale, port closed.

Down near Gibraltar you get the *levanter*, mostly in spring and early winter; towards the Balearic Islands, the *vendeval*, a west to south-westerly wind that occurs mostly in the winter months.

Snow is virtually unknown and fog occurs only occasionally in patchy form.

Public Holidays

1st January	Circumcision
6th January	The Three Kings
19th March	St. Joseph's Day or Spanish Fathers' Day
1st May	St. Joseph the Artisan's Day
29th June	St. Peter and St. Paul
18th July	Anniversary of the start of the Spanish Civil War 1936
12th October.. ..	Spanish National Day
1st November ..	All Saints' Day
8th December ..	The Immaculate Conception and Spanish Mothers' Day
25th December ..	Christmas Day

also Palm Sunday, Maundy Thursday, Good Friday, Easter Sunday, Ascension Day and Corpus Christi.

Hire Cars

Avis and Hertz are fairly well represented, also Atesa. Most travel agents are able to advise you.

Mail

You can buy stamps at Post Offices and tobacconists.
Letter boxes are painted silver and red, marked *Correos*.
Letters can be addressed to you at any Post Office and should give your name, c/o *Lista de Correos*, name of town and province. You should take your passport as identification.

Telephone

Mostly automatic.

Bull Fights

You may be tempted to go; if so, get a seat near the exit in case you have to leave in a hurry.

The cheapest seats, the *andanadas*, are in the sun, the best in the shade. The bullfighting season starts in March and ends in October. They usually take place on Sundays and public holidays.

Six bulls are killed, two by each of the matadors. The senior matador is the one who leads the procession out into the middle of the ring at the beginning.

The three stages of the bull fight are (1) slightly damaging the bull by *picadores* on padded horses, (2) provocation of the bull by the placing of *banderillas* by *banderillos* and (3) the kill by the *matador*. The excitement and atmosphere of a bullfight is something to experience, particularly when a top-ranking *matador* is appearing.

Needs a vet's certificate.

Cats and dogs   For bringing cats and dogs into Spain from the UK it is necessary to have a British veterinary surgeon's certificate of health in duplicate which must be authorized by the Ministry of Agriculture, Food and Fisheries in Britain. Another certificate must be supplied testifying that the area in which the animal lives is free from animal disease and this is to come from the Animal Health Division, Exports Section of the Ministry of Agriculture, Food and Fisheries, Hook Rise, Tolworth, Surbiton, Surrey. These certificates must then be legalized by the Spanish Consulate at 3, Hans Crescent, London, S.W.1 who will charge for each document to be legalized.

Weights and Measures

litres		gals
1	=	0,22
2	=	0,44
3	=	0,66
4	=	0,88
5	=	1,10
6	=	1,32
7	=	1,54
8	=	1,76
9	=	1,98
10	=	2,20
15	=	3,30
20	=	4,40
30	=	6.60
40	=	8,80
50	=	11,00
100	=	22,00

kms		miles
1	=	0,62
2	=	1,24
3	=	1,86
4	=	2,48
5	=	3,11
6	=	3,73
7	=	4,35
8	=	4,97
9	=	5,59
10	=	6,21
15	=	9,32
20	=	12,43
30	=	18,64
40	=	24,85
50	=	31,07
100	=	62,14

kgs		lbs
0,435	=	1
0,907	=	2
1,360	=	3
1,814	=	4
2,268	=	5
2,721	=	6
3,175	=	7
3,628	=	8
4,082	=	9
4,535	=	10

Public Toilets

There are not very many in Spain; when you find them they are marked *Retrete* or *El Water*; for men *Hombres* or *Caballeros*; for women *Señores*. It is usual to use toilets in bars, cafes, restaurants, petrol stations.

6 Costa Brava

Distances Between Harbours

	from Port Vendres	*kms*
Port Bou		13
Port de la Selva		12
Cadaques		12
Rosas and Ampuriabrava		12
Estartit		22
Palamos		22
San Filiu de Guixols		12
Blanes		24
	to Arenys	24

Average temperatures:

	Jan	Feb	Mar	Apl	May	Jun	Jly	Aug	Sep	Oct	Nov	Dec
MAX	57	57	61	63	68	74	90	78	77	69	62	59
MIN	43	43	46	49	55	60	65	69	62	55	49	45

(*right*) Costa Brava.

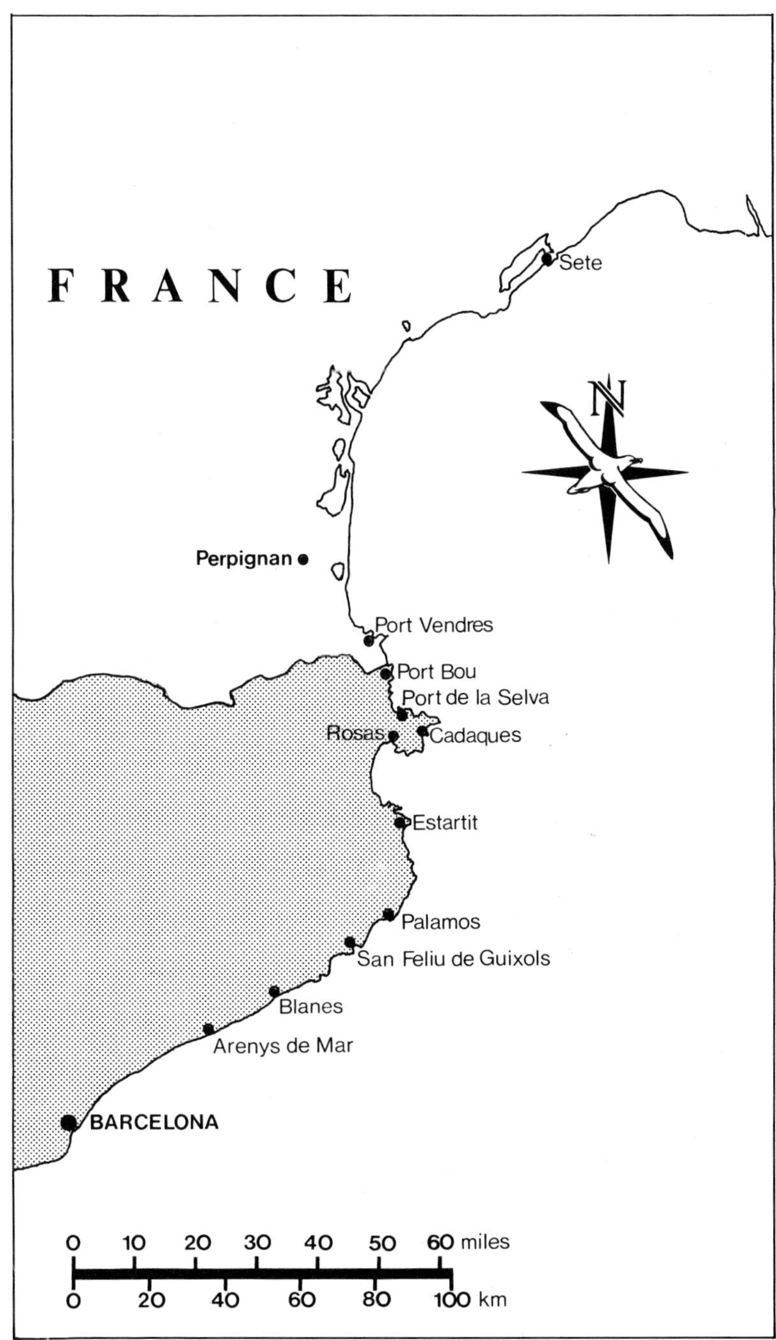

FRANCE
Sete
Perpignan
Port Vendres
Port Bou
Port de la Selva
Rosas
Cadaques
Estartit
Palamos
San Feliu de Guixols
Blanes
Arenys de Mar
BARCELONA
N
0 10 20 30 40 50 60 miles
0 20 40 60 80 100 km

Gerona can easily be visited by bus or train from harbours on the Costa Brava.

The Costa Brava is said to be one of the most beautiful coastlines in the world; extending from the French frontier ninety miles to Blanes it coincides with the Province of Gerona.

The Costas Brava and Dorada are part of Catalonia which is quite a special region of Spain, with its own language sharing a lot in common with Provençal, (although Spanish is the official language). The people are especially friendly to the British.

The attractions of its warm climate, rocks, golden sands, pine trees and countless coves have made the Costa Brava the number one holiday area on the Spanish mainland for British holiday-makers. At one time it was occupied mainly by painters and poets and today Salvador Dali has his house at Port Lligat.

Owing to the proximity of the Pyrenees it is not an area to winter in.

You should visit Gerona and will find either convenient bus or train services from most harbours.

A well known view of Gerona is of laundry hanging from the windows of the houses overlooking the River Oñar. It is a town full of interest and historic buildings, in particular the cathedral. If you are there at Easter you will see the penitents walking barefoot through the narrow streets, wearing black hoods and carrying candles.

June is probably the best month in which to visit the Costa Brava. The sea is warming up by mid-May and the crowds do not begin to appear until July; not that crowds will ever be visible on that shore line of Spain first visible through your binoculars. You will be scanning the dark and mountainous promontory culminating in Cape Creus.

Although Port Bou and Port de la Selva are on the Spanish side of this promontory we always seem to think of it as the natural boundary and not until we have passed the white tower, 300ft up on the summit of Cape Creus, do we feel that we are really in Spanish waters. This tower is the first of many such distinctive towers in similar rugged settings that will attract the aim of your hand-bearing compass.

Rounding Cape Creus is a dramatic introduction to your Spanish venture. Once past, the bay of Rosas seems to open out in welcome.

Port Bou

Admiralty Chart 1804 (pop: 2000)

Port Bou is a small, circular harbour and is not really of much interest to the yachtsman except as an emergency shelter.

It was once a small fishing village but has become an important Customs post between France and Spain.

It is dominated by railway sheds and is rather drab and uninteresting.

Distances:
to Barcelona 175k
to Gerona 75k

Port Bou.

Port De La Selva

Admiralty Chart 1615 (pop: 900)

A natural harbour in the pleasant setting of a small bay but, although it is quite a picturesque fishing village it is not of much interest to the yachtsman.

There are some historic buildings and nearby is the Monastery of San Pedro de Roda, 11thC and the ruined castle of San Salvador.

Distances:
to Barcelona 170k
to Gerona 70k

Port de la Selva

PORT SELVA

Church,- Lat. 42° 20′ 11″ N. Long. 3° 12′ 10″ E.

Mag. Var.ⁿ 4°50′W. (1964) decreasing about 7′ annually

10 Cables or
1 Sea Mile (6074 f.t)

Natural Scale $\frac{1}{18,222}$

TRUE NORTH

Cape Vol
La Musclera
Sernella Pt
La Musclera
Playa Sola de Sernella
La Cadena
Playa Coloma
Moll de La Vall
Playa de La Vall
Cap d'eterra
La Riumera
Playa den Pere Blei
Playa den Taita
Larolo Pt
Niell R.k
Playa de la Ribera

Creu Pt
Conill Cove
Pedrera
Playa Alpas
French Pt
Tamariua Cove
Volno
M.t Carbonera 390
M.t Mares 292
PORT SELVA
Lifeboat
Timba Pt
Old Church
M.t Forcas
M.t Victor 640
Els Corrals
Mill
Era

M.t Dijous 846

ort de la Selva.

Cadaques

Admiralty Charts 1615, 1804   (pop: 1200)

A deep water anchorage situated in a deep defile in the
rocks. The first impression of a jewel-like setting is not sustained
on rowing ashore.

It is little more than a straggling fishing village set around
a small bay, with white houses clustered against the background
of dark mountains.

The 16thC church has an altarpiece of Spanish baroque
workmanship. In the Town Hall is a collection of contemporary
paintings.

You should not go ashore here with the thought of exploring
further inland for it is most inaccessible.

Distances:

to Barcelona 169k
to Gerona 69k

Cadaques.

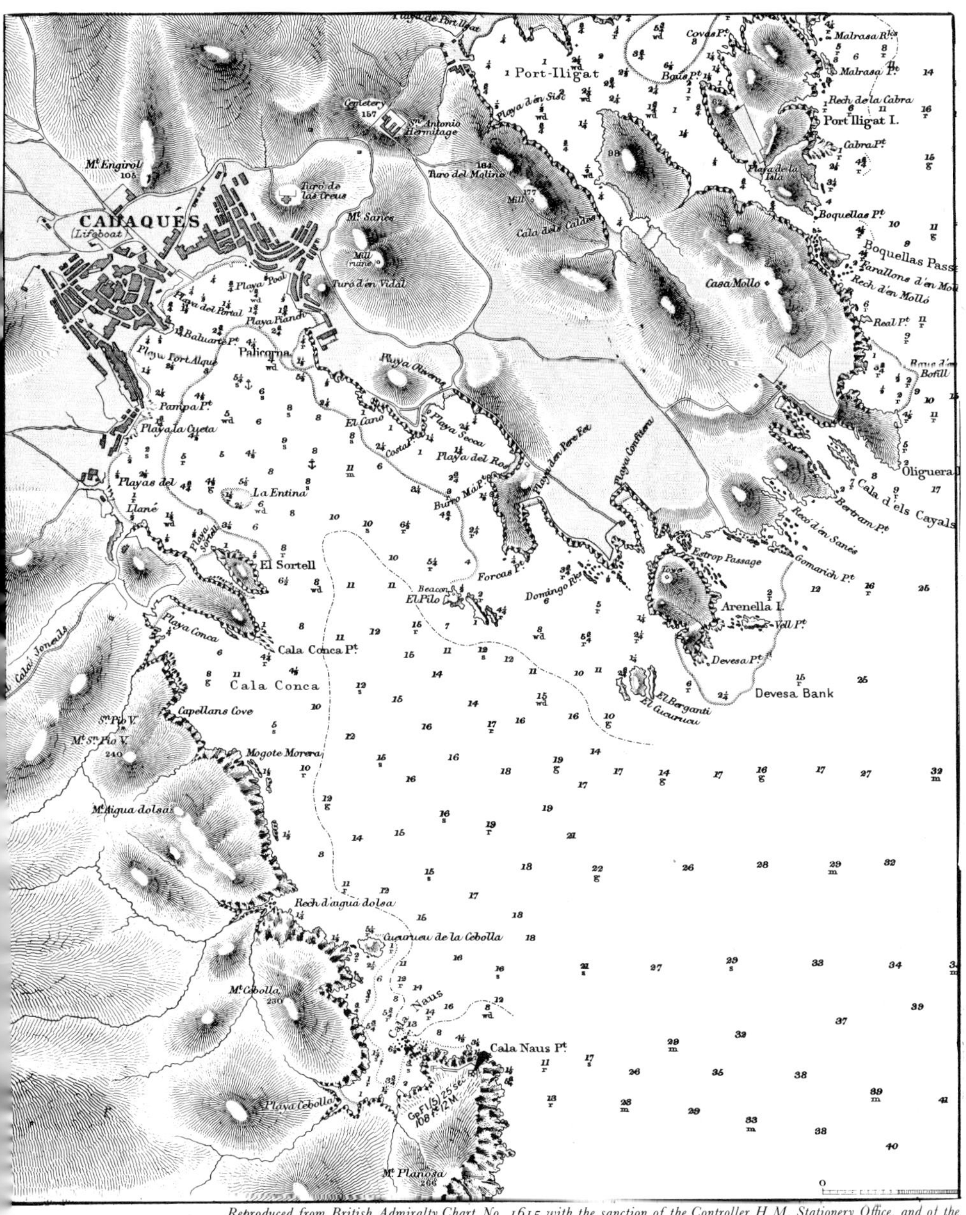

Reproduced from British Admiralty Chart No. 1615 with the sanction of the Controller H.M. Stationery Office, and of the Hydrographer of the Navy.

Rosas

Admiralty Chart 1615   (pop: 3000)

A fishing village that is developing as a holiday resort but the hotels are well away from the harbour. There is a small Club Nautico on the quay which is to starboard as you enter the bay and just before the town. It is convenient to tie up here, subject to the requirements of the fishing boats that return each evening.

There is a well known fish auction here and a Sunday market.

Good shops and restaurants are only a short walk from the quay.

Just beyond the town is the yacht harbour of Ampuriabrava —see page 71.

Distances:
to Barcelona 157k
to Gerona 57k

The quay, Rosas.

Rosas-Ampuriabrava

Admiralty Chart 1615

The entrance is difficult to discern at first for the projecting stonework of the moles blends in with the long beach; and when you discover the gap in the sand you see that quite a smart manoeuvre is necessary to enter. From the port-hand mole a projecting finger extends at right angles and you have to round this, quite tricky when there is an onshore wind.

But once inside you make for the tower and you are then in what is advertised as Europe's largest centre for watersports. There are inland harbours connected by eight miles of canals, alongside which are the splendid properties for sale (the *raison d'être* for Ampuriabrava), plus a hotel, restaurant, supermarket etc.

Ampuriabrava.

Estartit

Admiralty Chart 1804

A fishing port protected by a breakwater; rapidly growing in popularity as a holiday resort, the attraction being the miles of gently sloping sands, considered to be the most attractive on the Costa Brava.

The actual 'town' is hardly more than one street of souvenir shops and it is more a place for the holidaymaker than the yachtsman.

Market Thursday.

Distances:

to Barcelona 142k
to Gerona 45k

Palamos

Admiralty Chart 1391   (pop: 6000)

Quite an important commercial and fishing port at the north end of a large and beautiful bay.

The town is pleasant and quite small; a good selection of shops is within easy walking distance of the harbour.

The fish auction is held in the large building at the end of the quay.

Museum; ancient pottery, modern art.

Some tourism but not overwhelming; apart from this Palamos relies upon fishing and the cork industry.

Visiting yachtsmen are welcomed at the Club Nautico Costa Brava where all facilities are available plus a pleasant restaurant and open air swimming pool.

Distances:

to Barcelona 120k

to Gerona 44k

Club Nautico Costa Brava at the foot of the long breakwater in Palamos.

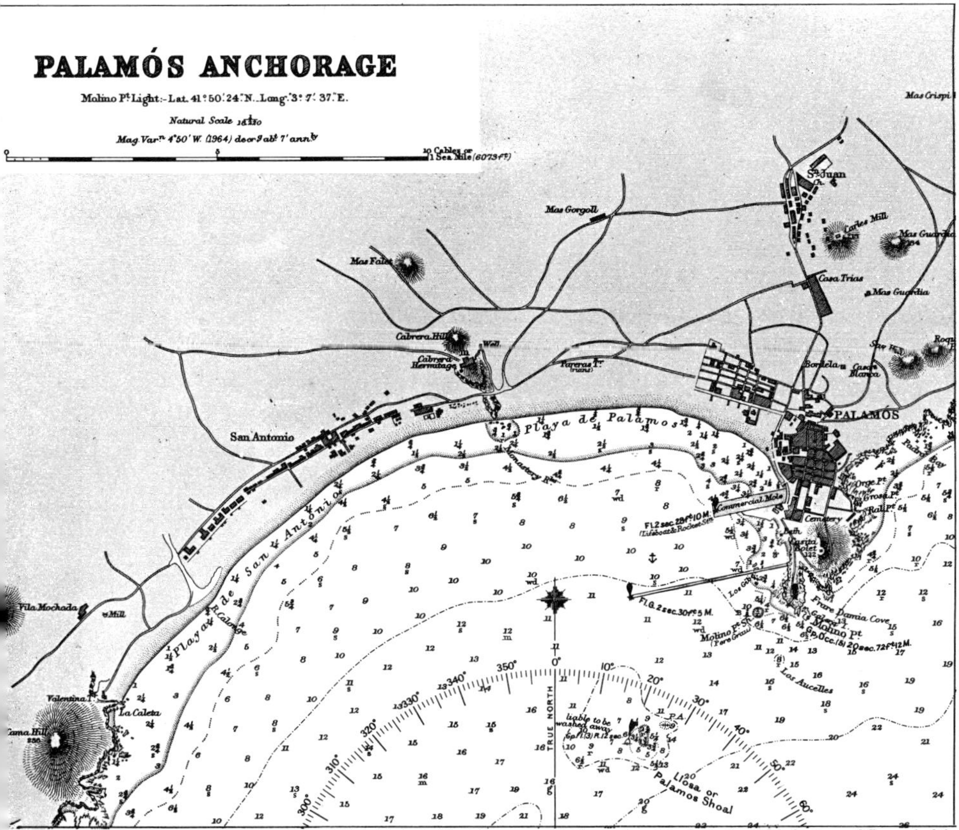

PALAMÓS ANCHORAGE

Molino Pt Light:- Lat. 41° 50′ 24″ N., Long. 3° 7′ 37″ E.

Natural Scale 1:18150

Mag. Varⁿ 4° 50′ W. (1964) decrⁿg abt 7′ annˡʸ

Reproduced from British Admiralty Chart No. 1391 with the sanction of the Controller H.M. Stationery Office, and of the Hydrographer of the Navy.

Palamos Anchorage.

Palamos town to the northwards of the Commercial Mole.

San Feliu De Guixols

Admiralty Chart 1391   (pop: 9000)

The largest town on the Costa Brava, a dignified town, clean and pleasant, situated in the middle of a beautiful bay and protected by a breakwater.

Not a predominantly holiday resort.

The small town is rather quaint; it is claimed that it has authentic Spanish atmosphere. There are smart shops convenient to the harbour, markets, bars, nightclubs and a bullring.

The Club Nautico San Feliu de Guixols welcomes visiting yachts and provides facilities, from 15 May to 30 September.

Distances:
    to Barcelona 106k
    to Gerona 35k

San Feliu de Guixols.   (*right*) San Feliu de Guixols anchorage.

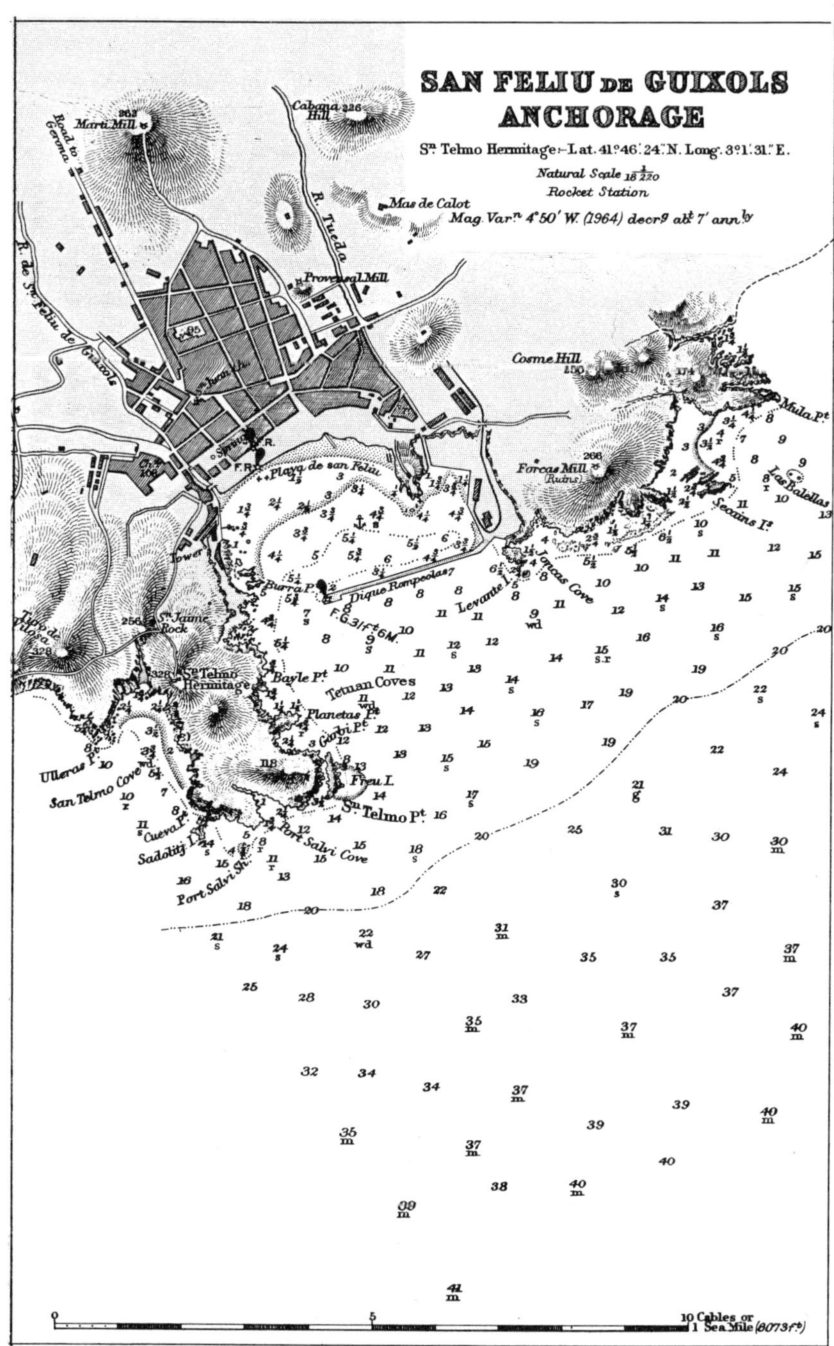

SAN FELIU DE GUIXOLS ANCHORAGE
Sᵗ Telmo Hermitage:-Lat. 41°46'.24".N. Long. 3°1'.31".E.
Natural Scale 1/18 220
Rocket Station
Mag. Varⁿ 4°50' W. (1964) decrg abᵗ 7' annᵗ
Road to Gerona
Marti Mill
Cabana Hill
Mas de Calot
R. Tueda
R. de Sᵗ Feliu de Guixols
Provençal Mill
Cosme Hill
Mula Pᵗ
Forcas Mill (Ruins)
Las Balellas
Secains Iˢ
Playa de san Feliu
Burra Pᵗ
Dique Rompeolas
Levante I.
Joncas Cove
Pᵗ de Hilosa
Sᵗ Jaime Rock
Sᵗ Telmo Hermitage
Bayle Pᵗ
Tetuan Coves
Planetas Pᵗ
Giabi Pᵗ
Freu I.
Sᵗ Telmo Pᵗ
Ulleras Pᵗ
San Telmo Cove
Cueva I.
Sadolitj I.
Port Salvi Sᵗ
Port Salvi Cove
10 Cables or 1 Sea Mile (6073 fᵗ)

Blanes

Admiralty Chart 1391   (pop: 9000)

A pleasant, old, small town situated at the foot of a hill by the River Tordera. There is a long beach and wide promenade, the streets are clean, or perhaps the whiteness of the houses accents their cleanliness.

There are shops of all kinds quite near to the harbour where mooring stern-to on the quay is the most convenient.

Blanes has one of the largest fishing fleets on the coast but the fishing boats do not seem to intrude on the yacht mooring area.

On the quay is an aquarium exhibiting a selection of Mediterranean fish.

Above, on the cliffs, is a botanical garden covering acres; guide books are available in English and describe some of the 3000 plants.

Blanes is not too crowded with holidaymakers and is a pleasant little place in which to tie up.

Distances:
    to Barcelona 63k
    to Gerona 40k

Blanes.   (*right*) Blanes Bay.

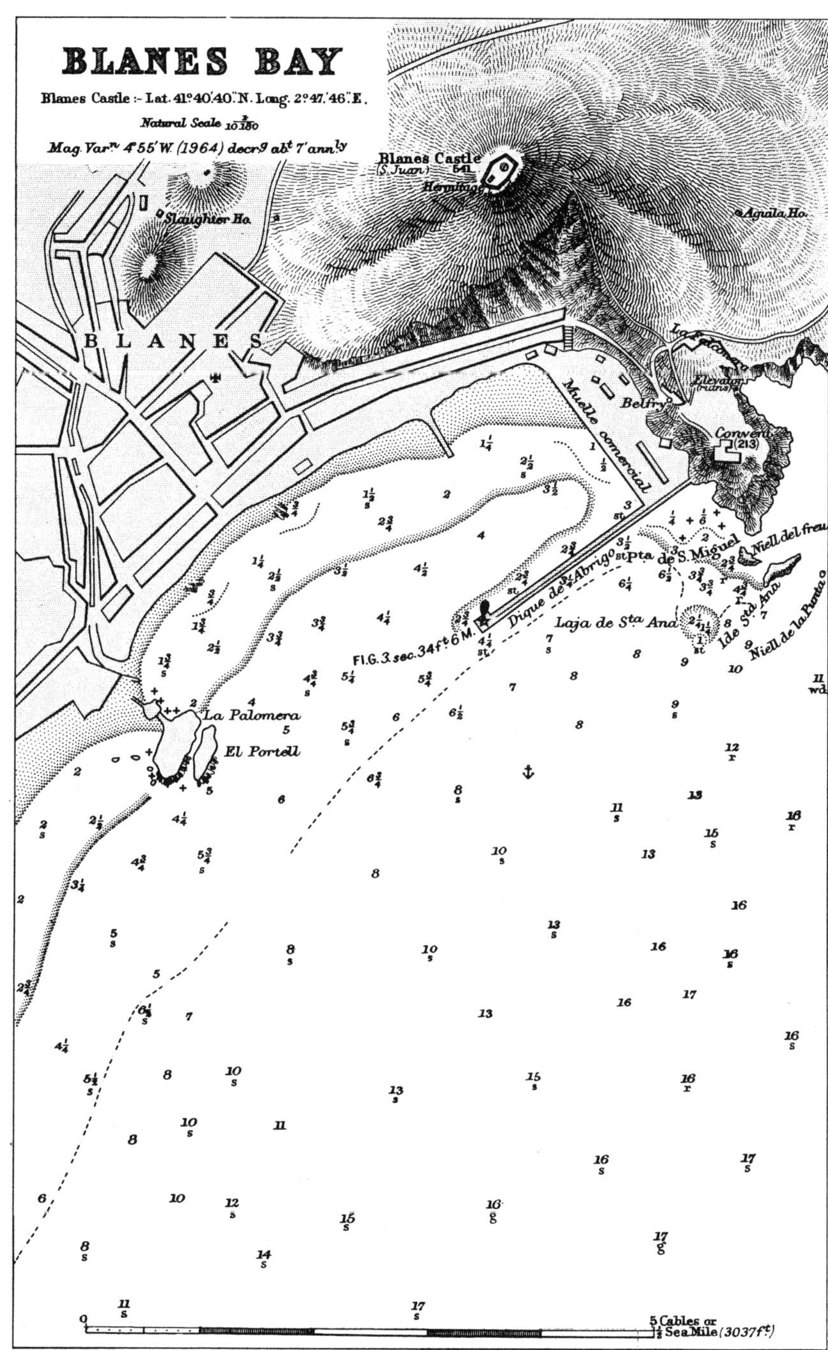

BLANES BAY
Blanes Castle :- Lat. 41°40'40" N. Long. 2°47'46" E.
Natural Scale 1/10180
Mag. Var.ⁿ 4°55'W. (1964) decrg abt 7' annⁿy
Blanes Castle
(S. Juan)
Hermitage
Slaughter Ho.
Aguila Ho.
BLANES
Muelle comercial
Belfry
Elevator (ruins)
Convent (213)
La Palomera
El Portell
FI.G. 3 sec. 34 ft 6 M.
Dique de Abrigo
Pta de S. Miguel
Niell del freu
Laja de Sta Ana
Ido Sta Ana
Niell de la Punta
0
5 Cables or
½ Sea Mile (3037 ft)

7 Costa Dorada

Distances Between Harbours:

	from Blanes	*Kms*
Arenys de Mar		24
Badalona		28
Barcelona		7
Garraf		11
Vallcarca		5
Villanueva y Geltru		9
Tarragona		35
Cambrils		22
Ebro Delta		22
Alfaques		27

Average temperatures:

	Jan	Feb	Mar	Apl	May	Jun	Jly	Aug	Sep	Oct	Nov	Dec
MAX	56	58	61	65	70	77	83	83	77	70	61	56
MIN	43	45	49	52	58	65	70	70	66	59	52	47

(*right*) Costa Dorada.

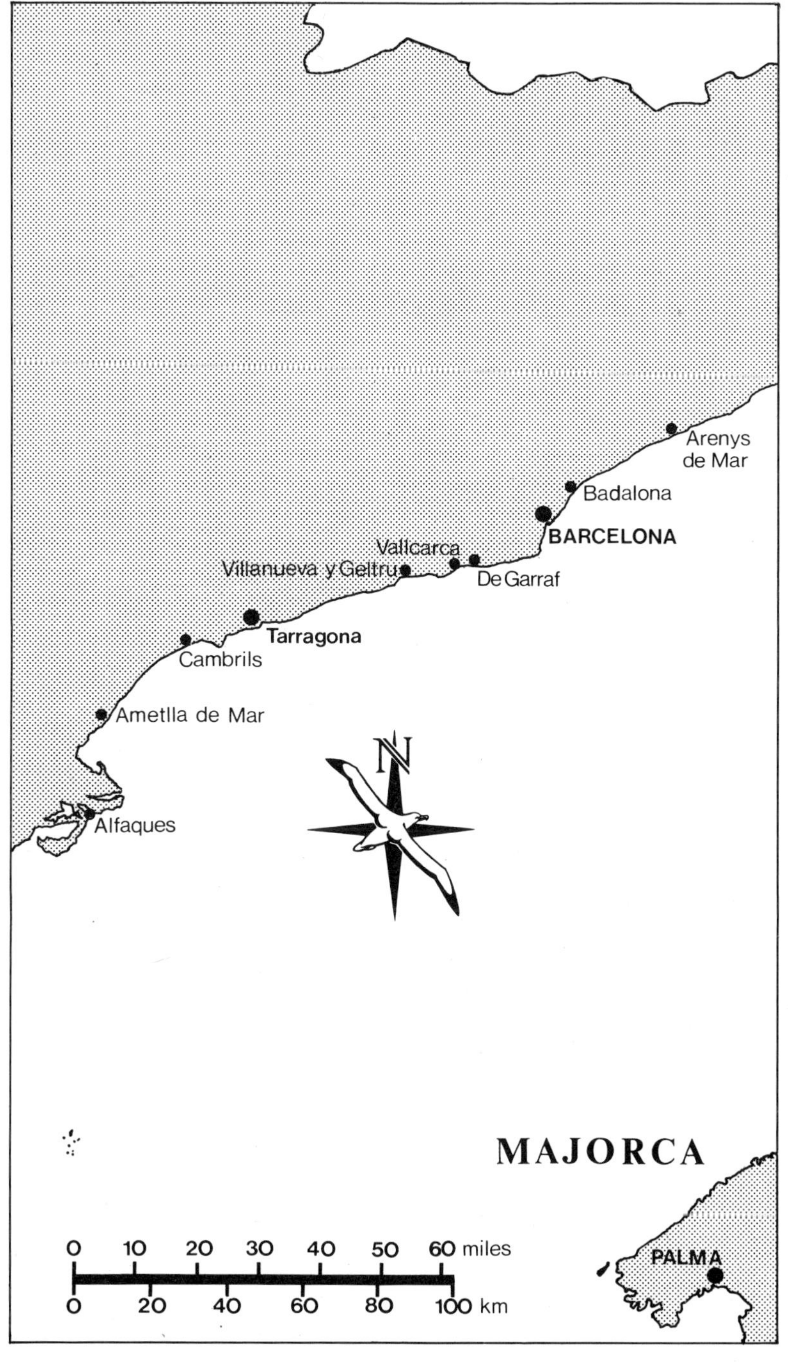

Arenys
de Mar
Badalona
BARCELONA
Vallcarca
Villanueva y Geltru
De Garraf
Tarragona
Cambrils
Ametlla de Mar
Alfaques
N
MAJORCA
PALMA
0 10 20 30 40 50 60 miles
0 20 40 60 80 100 km

Round the corner from Blanes you can see by the change in the character of the scenery where the Costa Brava ends and the Costa Dorada begins; the ruggedness gives way to an enormous beach, fifty kilometres long, stretching all the way to Barcelona.

Before Barcelona, only Arenys de Mar is of interest to the yachtsman and since both are 'marina stops' it will be expensive to linger for long in this area. Sometimes, in the summer months, it is not possible to get into the marina at Arenys at all; apart from the interest of visiting the first Spanish marina down the coast there is nothing much ashore here and you would do better to save your marina charges until to get to Barcelona. Here you will want to stay and will consider the marina charges well worthwhile.

After Barcelona the picturesque coast of Garraf precedes the smooth sand of the Province of Tarragona; from Tarragona there is little of interest in the rest of the Costa Dorada which now recedes as you set a course to clear Cape Tortosa.

Neither is there anything of interest immediately inland of the Costa Dorada but Barcelona is enough; the road and railway to it run parallel to the sea.

(*left*) Columbus and his ship in Barcelona.

Arenys De Mar

Admiralty Chart 310

The main attraction is the marina complex; outside of this
there is nothing much of interest in the town which is cut off
from the harbour by a railway and a busy main road. You get
to it from the marina through an underpass.

Because of its geographic position, sheltered by mountains,
Arenys has a temperate year-round climate.

The Club Nautico Arenys de Mar can only be described
as grand, (there are *two* club secretaries). If you enter this luxury
in your usual going-ashore gear the uniformed servants will not
raise an eyebrow but you may feel a bit self-conscious.

As you enter the harbour you will be noticed for it is small
and dominated by the Club Nautico; drifting up to the marina
berths you will be shown where to tie up and asked how long
you propose to stay. The notice that is handed to you 'welcomes
you sincerely', includes a short questionnaire for your completion
and states the tariff:—

	Daily rates
6,00 × 2,00m	100 pesetas
8,50 × 2,50m	150
11,00 × 3,00m	200
14,00 × 3,50m	250
16,00 × 4,00m	350
18,00 × 4,25m	450

Arenys de Mar harbour.

If the marina is full you can try to tie up by the fishing boats on the wall opposite but look out for the underwater rocks and stones, (you can see them down through the water), as you come alongside.

There is a fair selection of shops in the town.

It is not easy to find a summer berth in Arenys de Mar.

The Club Nautico Arenys de Mar.

Badalona

Admiralty Chart 310

A brochure guide states 'beach unsuitable owing to industrial waste' and with the proximity of Campsa storage tanks, railway sheds, factories, pipe lines and a hideous background of industry, no yachtsman in his right mind would linger here when the grandeur of Barcelona is so near.

Distances:
to Barcelona 8k

In Barcelona you tie up right in the city.

Barcelona

Admiralty Chart 1195   (pop: 2 000 000)

Rounding the mole you proceed up through the dock area almost as far as you can go until you see masts, turning in left the marina berths are then ahead on your right hand. The big sign on the wall tells you which numbered berths to make for according to the size of your boat.

The Real Club Nautico de Barcelona is right in Barcelona, you walk ashore into the heart of the town. The club is friendly and hospitable to visiting yachtsmen and so very convenient; it seems no distance to stroll back to your boat from the club showers; no distance to wander to Los Caracoles for your inexpensive supper.

After your first free days at the Real Club Nautico the rate is 100 pesetas a day up to 8m LOA rising up to 500 pesetas a

There is usually room here . . .

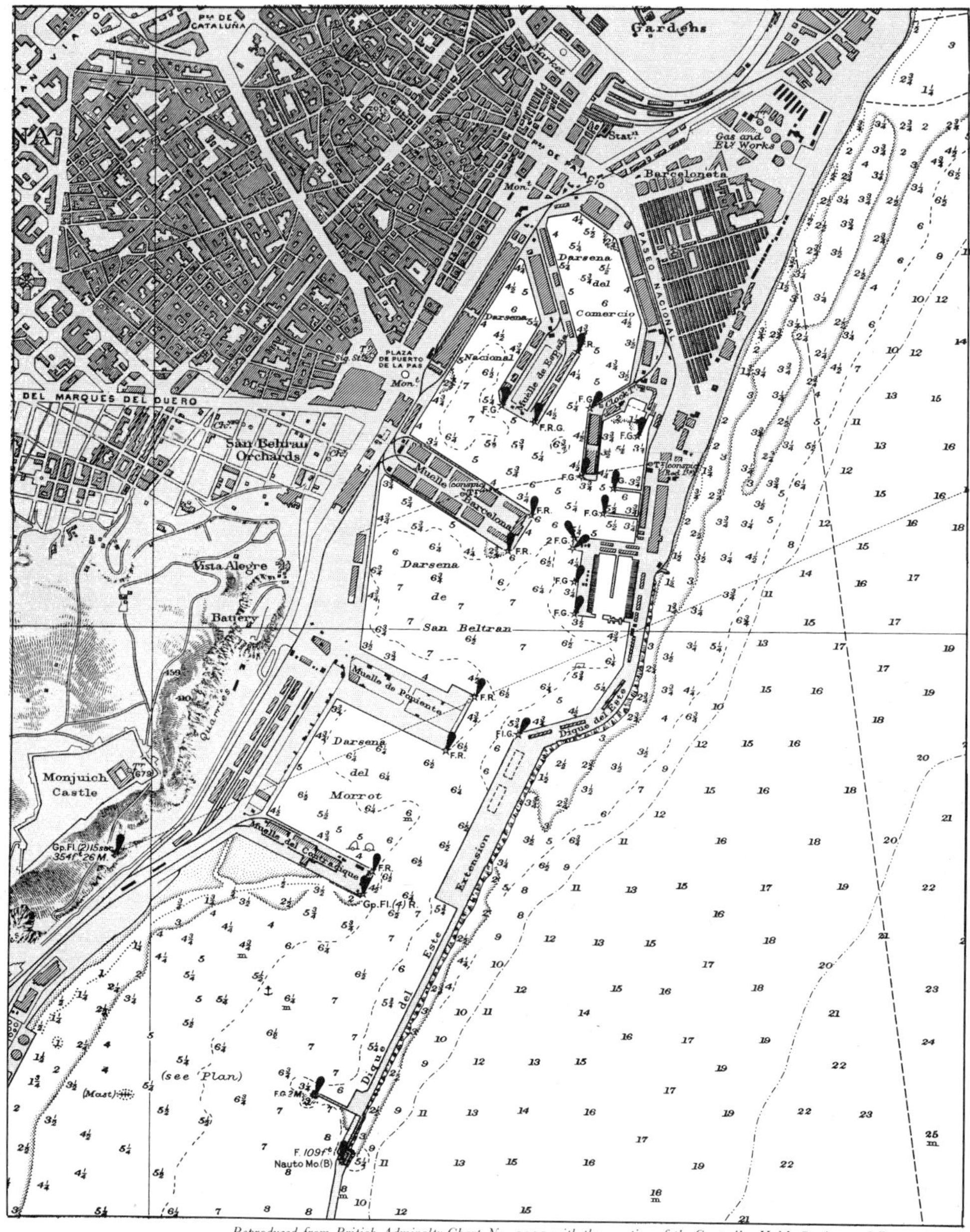

Barcelona Harbour.

day for 20m. You do not have to berth in the marina in Barcelona; we met a family who had wintered in their boat at a quayside berth allotted to them by the harbour master. This was understandable for a long stay but the marina is obviously much more agreeable and convenient.

The Port of Barcelona is completely artificial or man made. Out of the total lengths of quays of 10,390m commercial traffic uses 7051m, ships repairs 1731m, fishing 517m and sporting activities 1090m. From which you will note the relative importance of yachting to shipping and take care to keep out of the way of the big ships that use this port.

Across from the marina you will be interested to see the tall column atop of which stands Christopher Columbus; you can walk up or ride up inside and look down on the faithfully re-constructed, life-sized replica of the *Santa Maria* below, and possibly on your own little ship too. Another aerial view of your boat can be obtained from the little transporter cars that swing along on wires suspended over the city.

There is so much to see and do in this prosperous city, the centre of which, the Place de Cataluna, is only a short walk from the marina.

If you are fond of museums the Picasso Museum and the Museum of Modern Art are a warp's length away; scattered around the city are more than twenty museums, archeological, numismatic, musical, maritime, philatelic, military, also a zoo and an aquarium. The necessary transport to get to them, either bus or taxi, is cheap.

Female members of the crew should be kept away from the Ramblas, the Paseo de Gracia and the Avenida José Antonio for these are the fashionable shopping areas and temptations might arise to waste money that could be better spent on essentials like cigars, pipe tobacco and wine.

It is likely that you will find other English-speaking yacht owners here. We usually do. It is an altogether delightful place and you will not want to leave.

De Garraf

Admiralty Chart 310

A very small harbour formed by two moles; there has been some silting up and entry should not be attempted without local guidance. Ashore there is nothing except a bijou yacht club, a few small hotels dominated by the constant roar of main road traffic above. There are no shops.

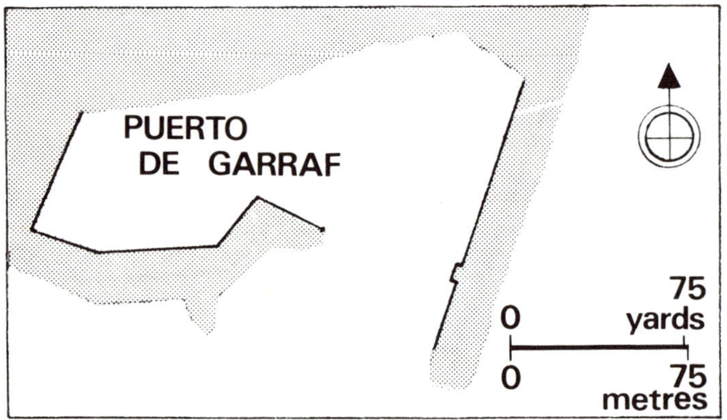

Vallcarca

Admiralty Chart 310

Although shown on maps as a harbour this is, in fact, a cement works and the attractions for the yachtsman can be imagined. There is a long mole but part of the harbour is privately maintained. The cement works are prominent and the surrounding vegetation is grey and sad.

Villanueva Y Geltru

Admiralty Chart 310

This harbour is formed by two moles and is divided into an outer and an inner harbour. The fishing boats and commercial traffic are segregated and visiting yachts may moor near the Club Nautico or stern-to on the club pontoons if there is room.

The pleasant town is only a short distance away.

The Museo Balaguer, in the La Geltru castle built between the 12th and 15thC, has a number of treasures of interest; amongst them 'Annunciation' by El Greco, a collection of 5000 coins and 3000 medals.

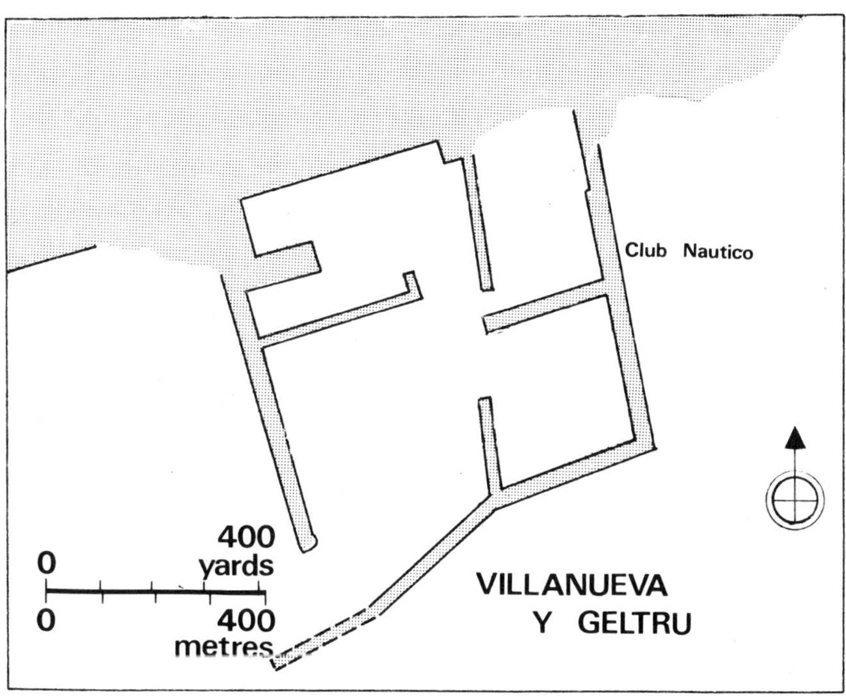

Tarragona

Admiralty Chart 344   (pop: 50 000)

The ochre-stone buildings of Tarragona seem to rise up from the sea and the surrounding countryside of olive trees and vineyards. One of the most interesting towns in Spain it has the advantage of possessing a friendly Club Nautico where visiting yachts are made welcome plus a good public jetty where a long stay may be contemplated at small cost.

Entering the harbour it is wise to secure first to this jetty and to stroll from here round to the adjacent Club Nautico to ascertain the moorings position.

There is a large yacht yard here where boats may be slipped and repairs undertaken; unfortunately the harbour is bounded by a number of factories which sometimes emit a disagreeable smoke from their chimneys.

The harbour is quite a long way from the town but there is a frequent bus service from opposite the Club Nautico. In the immediate vicinity there are shops where daily wants may be obtained but it is a typical 'port area' and rather uninviting on that account.

Tarragona is an old city—Augustus and Hadrian lived here when it was the capital of Roman Spain—and the splendid Gothic cathedral has many Roman remains.

Muller
Puerta de Francoli
Plaza de los Infantes
Calle Real
Calle del Leon
Calle del Mar
Plaza de Olozaga
San Pedro
Yacht Club
Warehouse
Workshops
N.º4
N.º3
N.º2
N.º1
Estacion de Reus
Police Stn
Health Office
Muelle de Pescadores
Muelle   de   Costa
Customs
Slipway
Shipyard
Rio Francoli
Muelle de Levente
Workshops
DARSENA
Muelle Transversal or
Espigón del Francoli
Gp.Occ.(2)R.6sec.
36ft.4M.
Occ.G.4sec.
35ft.4M.
Muelle Paralelo
al de Costa
Contradique
Gp.Fl.(2)R.6sec.
46ft.6M.
ANTEPUERTO
Escollera del Este
LOS CA
Health Or
Nuevo Dique de Levante
Banco del Sagrista
(rock, covered with sand)
330°
320°
310°
300°
290°
280°
270°

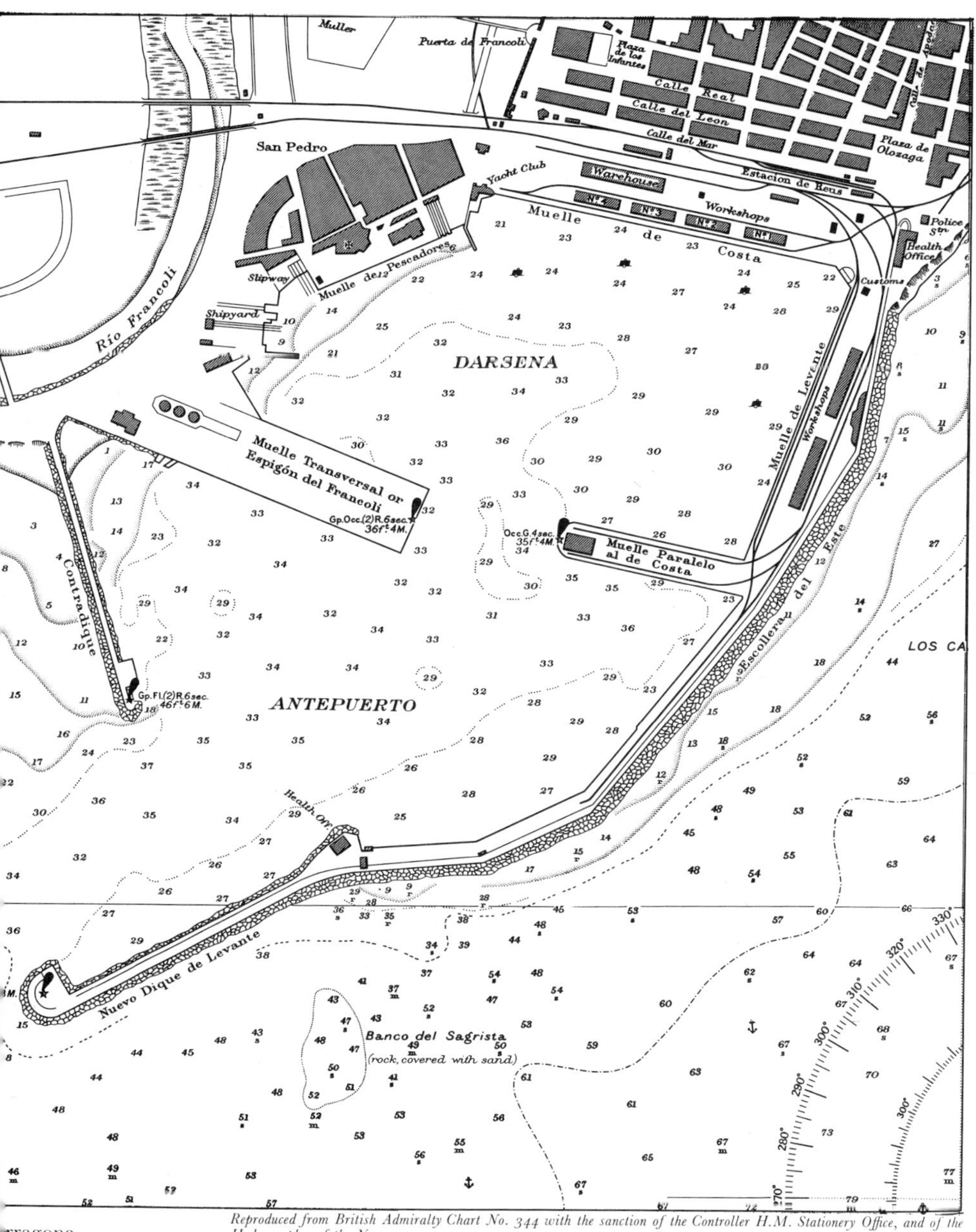

rragona.

Cambrils

Admiralty Chart 310   (pop: 2000)

A splendid little harbour with pontoon jetties for stern-to mooring.

The Club Nautico de Cambrils has berths for 200 boats and makes visiting yachts most welcome. All facilities are available and the fishing boats are segregated.

Immediately adjacent to the harbour is a shore line of shops and a beach of fine sand.

Distances:

to Tarragona 15k

(*below and right*) Cambrils.

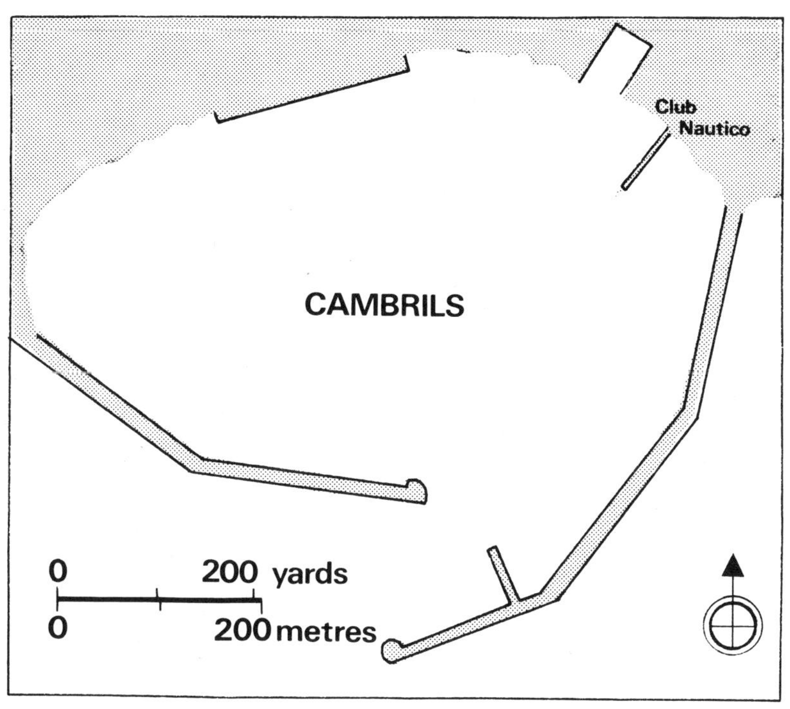

Club
Nautico
CAMBRILS
0
200 yards
0
200 metres

The Ebro Delta

Puerto Del Fangar
Puerto De Los Alfaques
San Carlos De La Rapita
Admiralty Charts 310, 1320, 1571

Leaving Tarragona most yachts set a course from Cape Salou to give a wide berth to Cape Tortosa and the shoreline of the Ebro Delta which, as the chart confirms, is continually advancing seawards.

The desolate and stagnant triangle of Alfaques de Tortosa, (the Ebro Delta), has nothing of interest for the cruising yachtsman except shelter, for 'any port in a storm' is welcome, even Fangar and Alfaques.

In the event of weather deteriorating on approaching the cape there is shelter from all directions in the so called Puerto del Fangar but ashore all is desolation. The next nearest place on your chart this side of Cape Tortosa is Ametlla De Mar which is a small fishing boat harbour with no particular facility for visiting yachts.

Cape de Tortosa marks the main channel to the River Ebro but depths here are uncertain due to continuous shoaling off the entrance to the river. Although it is the principal river in the eastern part of Spain there is a shallow bar and shifting shoals at its mouth and you would be unwise to attempt an entry without a pilot. The town of Tortosa lies 25 miles up from the mouth of the river.

The Ebro Delta . . . ashore all is desolation.

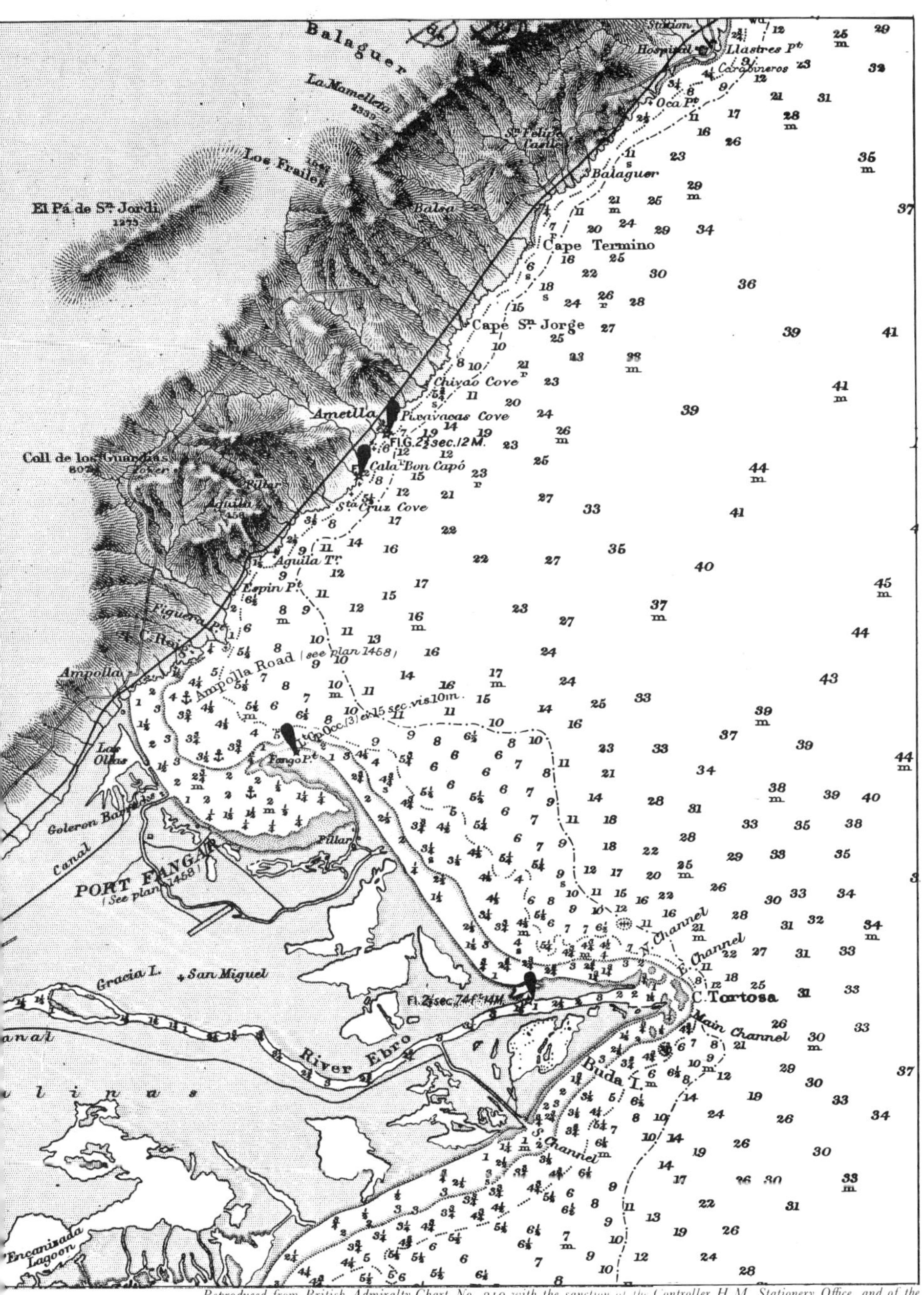

Balaguer
La Mamellera
Los Frailes
El Pá de Sta Jordi
Coll de los Guardias
Ametlla
Chivao Cove
Piravacas Cove
Cala Bon Capó
Sta Cruz Cove
Aguila Tr
Espin Pt
Figuera Pt
C. Roi
Ampolla
Ampolla Road (see plan 1458)
Fango Pt
Los Ollas
Goleron Bay
Canal
PORT FANGAL
(See plan 1458)
Pillar
Gracia I.
San Miguel
River Ebro
Buda I.
Encanisada Lagoon
Station
Hospital
Llastres Pt
Carabineros
Oca Pt
St Felipe Castle
S Balaguer
Cape Termino
Cape Sn Jorge
V. Channel
E. Channel
C. Tortosa
Main Channel
S Channel

Proceeding south past Cape Tortosa the Punta de la Baña should be given a wide berth for, as has already been mentioned, the coastline is constantly extending seawards.

Although the Puerto de los Alfaques is so named it possesses nothing except a sheltered anchorage and not completely so, for it can be quite choppy in here when the wind is anywhere in the north.

Proceeding into Puerto de los Alfaques between Punta de la Senieta and Punta del Galacho you will see a mole ahead; rounding this the small inner harbour of San Carlos de la Rapita will then appear to your left, protected by a mole and a breakwater.

San Carlos is mainly a fishing boat harbour but there is a Club Moto Nautico near which one can tie up or, alternatively, to the left on coming in. The immediate vicinity of the harbour is uninspiring and the traders in the only street seem to be mostly concerned with the sale of souvenirs, not surprising since it is the main Valencia–Barcelona highway.

Apparently San Carlos was founded by Charles III with the intention of making it a prosperous trading port. A beautiful square of grandiose design is all that remains.

You can get good prawns in this area. Alcanar, nine miles away, is famous for the Dublin Bay variety.

The River Ebro.

Amposta
Rio Ebro
Canal
a Rio Ebro
968
Encañizada Lagoon
Granada Mt
2290
Pascual Mt
2506
S. Carlos de la Rapita
Guardiola Tr
Sanieta Pt
Gp.Occ.(1+4) 20 sec.11 M.
Mt
211
Galachero Canal
Fango Pt
Depths are less than charted
G.Fl.(2)R.8M.
Playa del Trabucador
Galacho Pt
Fl.G.
Salinas de la Trinidad
Fl.5 M.
CAUTION
The shore line has advanced
to the S.&W.& the depths in
the vicinity have decreased.
P.A.
C. Alcanar
Cape Baña Gp.Occ.(3)15sec.
11 59f.13M.
PORT ALFAQUES
(see plan 1571)

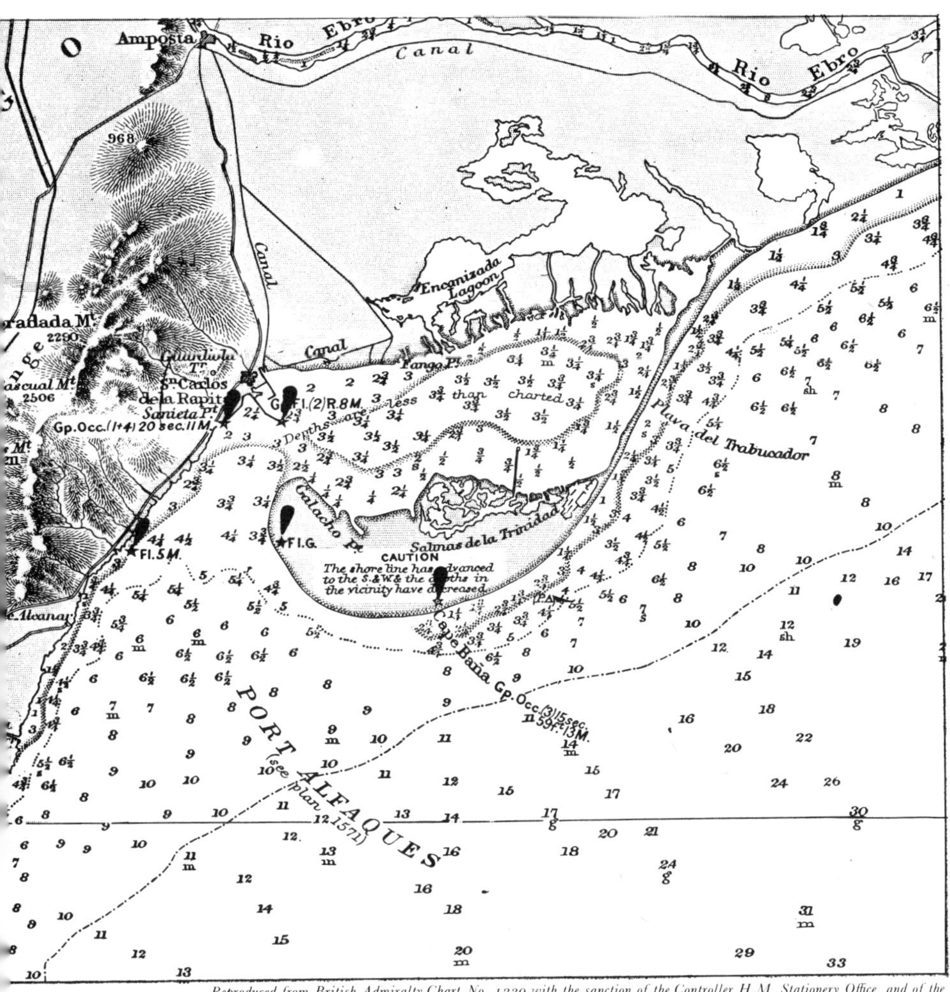

rt Alfaques.

8 Costa Del Azahar

Distances between Harbours

Alfaques to	Kms
Vinaroz	24
Benicarlo	7
Peniscola	7
Castellon	57
Burriana	24
Sagunto	26
Valencia	26
Cullera	32
Gandia	28
Denia	25

Average temperatures:

	Jan	Feb	Mar	Apl	May	Jun	Jly	Aug	Sep	Oct	Nov	Dec
MAX	59	61	65	68	74	79	84	84	81	74	66	61
MIN	43	43	47	50	56	61	66	68	65	59	50	45

(*right*) Costa del Azahar.

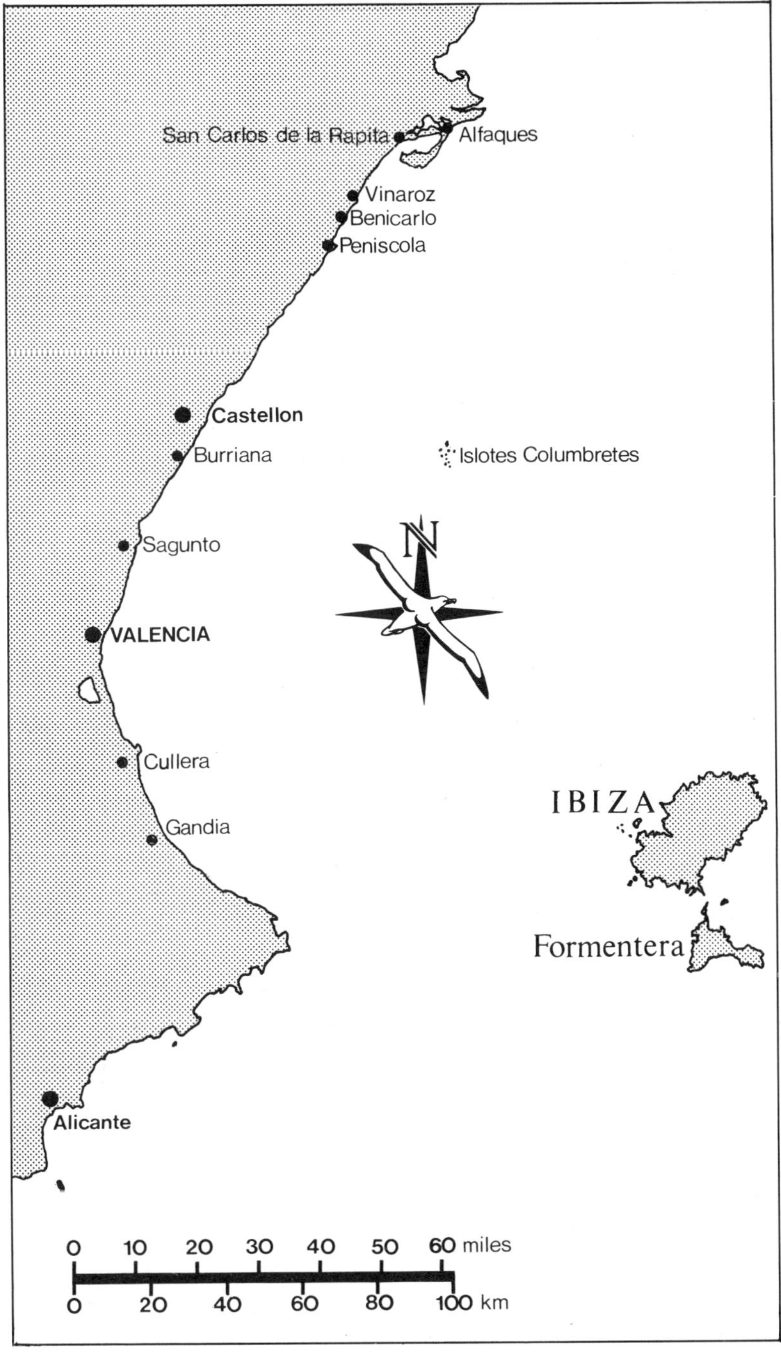

San Carlos de la Rapita
Alfaques
Vinaroz
Benicarlo
Peniscola
Castellon
Burriana
Islotes Columbretes
N
Sagunto
VALENCIA
Cullera
Gandia
IBIZA
Formentera
Alicante
0 10 20 30 40 50 60 miles
0 20 40 60 80 100 km

Down the Spanish Coast

The Costa del Azahar is a beautiful stretch of coastline; when you round Cape Tortosa and look towards the wide curve of the Gulf of Valencia you really feel that you are getting down towards the sunshine, as indeed you are.

A background of mountains prevents cold winds from reaching the Costa del Azahar. Everywhere along the whole length of the coast of Castellon and Valencia are orange and lemon groves.

What is known as the 'Levante' coast begins here at Castellon and as you cruise peacefully along in the sunshine you

Peniscola has an attractive fishing boat harbour and the castle of El Macho.

will want to be on your guard for a set of two or three knots in towards the land.

The Phoenician captains brought their ships to these interesting shores but there were not very many holidaymakers here then; not that this coast is overwhelmed, with the possible exception of Peniscola's ancient fortress in July and August.

You could plan your cruising schedule to be here in spring or autumn for the best combination of blissful seagoing and peaceful shore-going. Even in winter you may still be very comfortable here indeed.

Vinaroz

Admiralty Chart 1187   (pop: 13 000)

When the fishing boats are in they take up most of the room in this harbour but do not let this put you off for the fishermen are friendly and helpful.

There is a ship-breaking yard on the other side of the fishing quay and sheds but its presence is not obtrusive.

The town is a short walk from the harbour and it is pleasantly laid out with a garden-promenade; all sorts of shops are near, also an open vegetable market.

Famous for big langostinos, Vinaroz is first and foremost a fishing port and because of this you would not find it convenient to tie up here for any length of time.

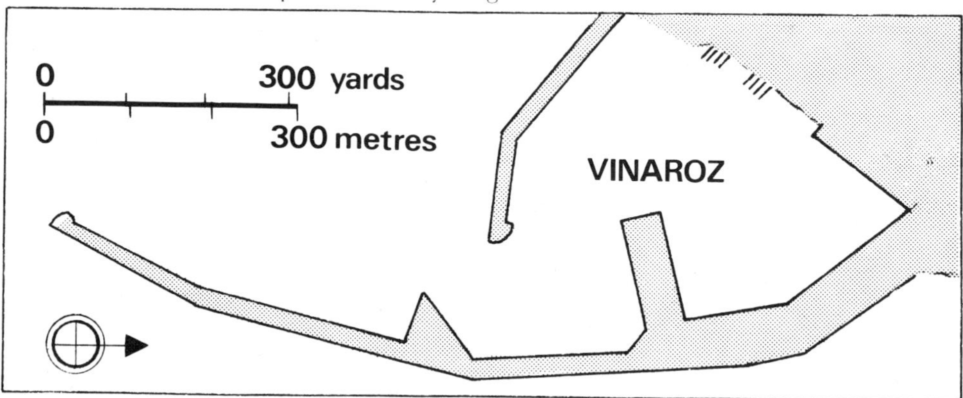

Vinaroz.

Benicarlo

Admiralty Chart 1320 (pop: 13 000)

A small fishing boat harbour. The fishing boats tie up to your left on entry, you anchor in the middle.

Looking through Benicarlo harbour entrance you can see the hill of Peniscola, reminding you that you should make this your next stop.

Benicarlo is quite an unpretentious little harbour with water and fuel available near the port and a good selection of shops nearby.

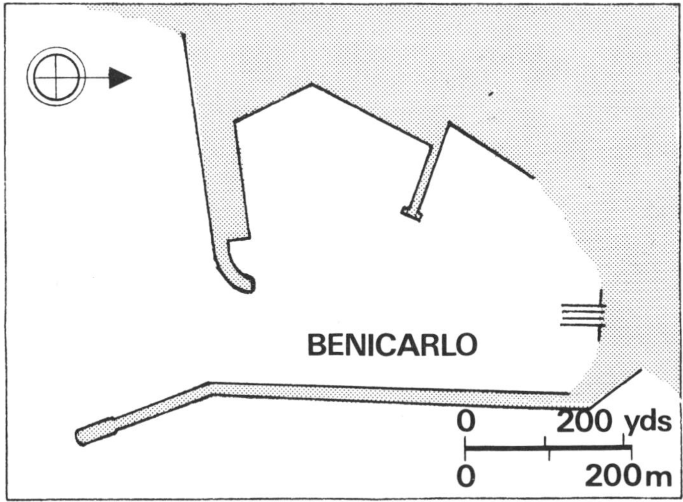

Benicarlo.

Peniscola

Admiralty Chart 1187   (pop: 2500)

An attractive fishing boat harbour; you should anchor in
the middle initially and examine the alongside possibilities for
your draft, (as, by now, you will probably be accustomed to
anyhow). Most yachts prefer the peace of lying at anchor here
and it is only a short row ashore.

You can get most provisions you need from the shops in the
quaint narrow streets and alleys. The big tourist attraction of
Peniscola is the Castle of El Macho, the 15thC refuge of Pope
Luna, or Papa Luna as Benedict XIII was called. Last of the
Popes of Avignon he set up his pontifical court in the castle. You
can still see his coat-of-arms by one of the gateways, also the
Basilica, the sacristy and Benedict's cross and chalice.

Peniscola gets crowded with tourists in July and August,
particularly.

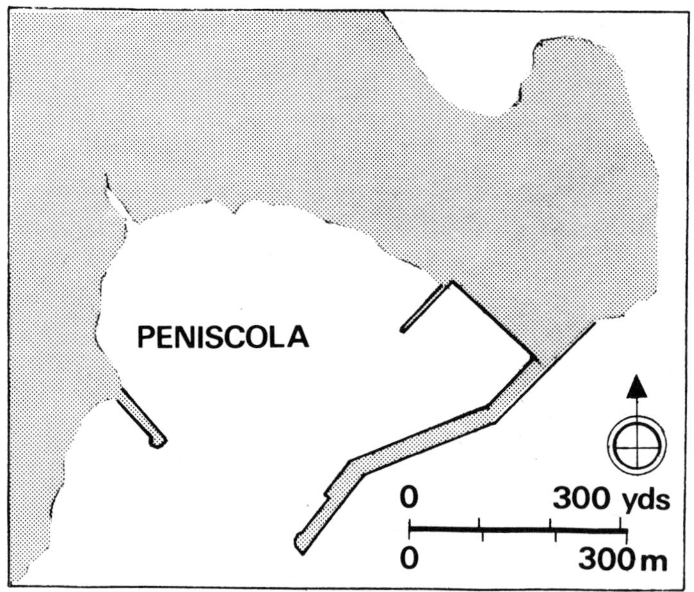

(right) Peniscola harbour.

Castellon

Admiralty Chart 1571   (pop: 87 000)

Castellon is a splendid place to visit, either for a short or a long stay. On entering the harbour you will see the large quay areas of the fishing fleet in their own harbour to your left, big ship quays and a ship-breaker's yard to your right and, straight ahead, the yacht club moorings of the hospitable Club Nautico. Until recently it was possible to moor stern-to right on to the club landing stage but now trots have been laid just off.

Visiting yachts have the use of the club showers, restaurant, bar, in fact all facilities; as with all clubs the facilities are more fully engaged by members at week-ends when there is dinghy racing etc.

The Club Nautico is at the Puerto del Grao de Castellon

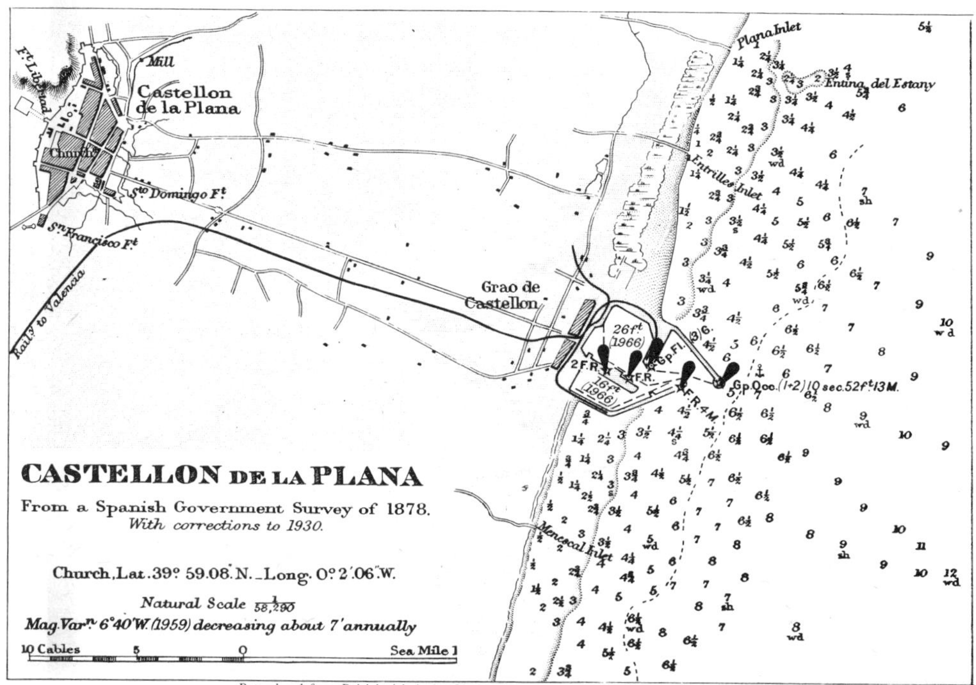

CASTELLON DE LA PLANA

From a Spanish Government Survey of 1878.
With corrections to 1930.

Church, Lat. 39° 59.08′ N. — Long. 0° 2′.06′ W.

Natural Scale $\frac{1}{58,290}$

Mag. Var.ⁿ 6° 40′ W. (1959) *decreasing about 7′ annually*

10 Cables   5   0   Sea Mile 1

and the attractive town of Castellon de la Plana, provincial
capital, is two miles away. A frequent bus service connects the
two and the bus stop is just outside the harbour gates.

It is a short bus ride with orange groves on either side, and
you are set down amidst the wide streets and well kept plazas of
the capital. The principal monument, dominating the countryside, is the 135ft Torre de las Campanas, the Bell Tower; the
cathedral church of Santa Maria preserves 14thC Gothic portals
and here you can see paintings of Francisco Ribalta; Zurbaran
paintings may be seen in the Convent of the Capuchines.

You do not have to take a bus ride to do your everyday
shopping for there are shops at El Grao within a short distance
of the harbour gates.

If you decide to visit the Islotes Columbretes (Chart 1458)
take a knowledgeable member of the Castellon Club Nautico
with you.

Castellon. The Club Nautico is the 4-storey building on the right.

Burriana

Admiralty Chart 1571   (pop: 23 000)

A breaker's yard predominates with biggish ships, usually aground, awaiting their end.

Fishing boats share the harbour and you should anchor in the middle; there is a small Club Nautico.

The port is some way from the pleasant town of Burriana which lies in a wide plain, surrounded by orange groves and good farmland.

There is a good selection of shops in the narrow streets of Burriana; but nothing to attract in the harbour area.

Burriana and (*right*) Sagunto.

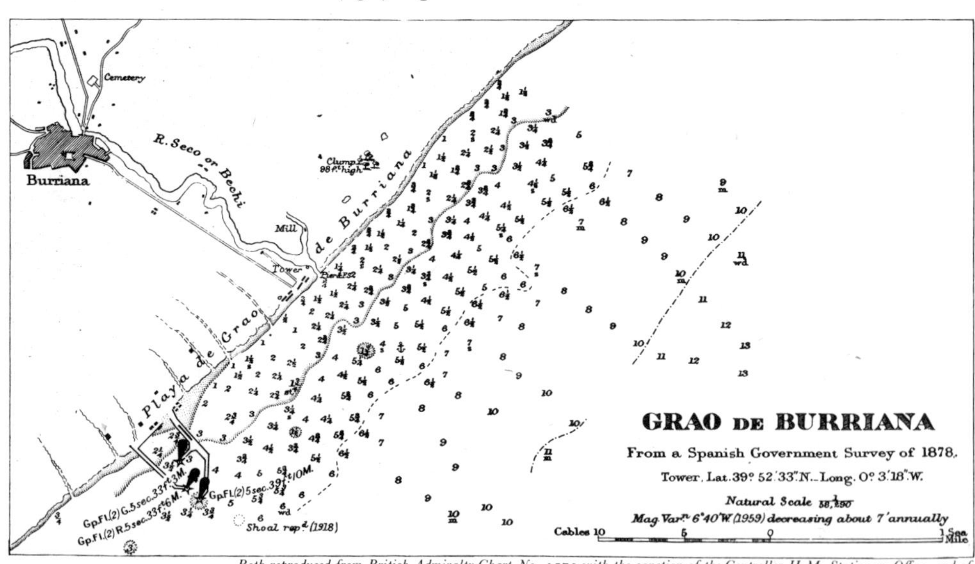

Both reproduced from British Admiralty Chart No. 1571 with the sanction of the Controller H.M. Stationery Office, and of the Hydrographer of the Navy.

Sagunto

Admiralty Chart 1320 (pop: 46 000)

The harbour of Sagunto is right in the middle of belching chimneys and obnoxious industry but it is still a harbour catering for the needs of shipping and there are shops in the port area.

The Sagunto of historic fame is 6k away, six hideous kilometres, unfortunately, but if you are determined to see one of the most notable Roman theatres in Spain, an archaeological museum with an Iberian stone bull and an Indian Bacchus you will, no doubt, persevere.

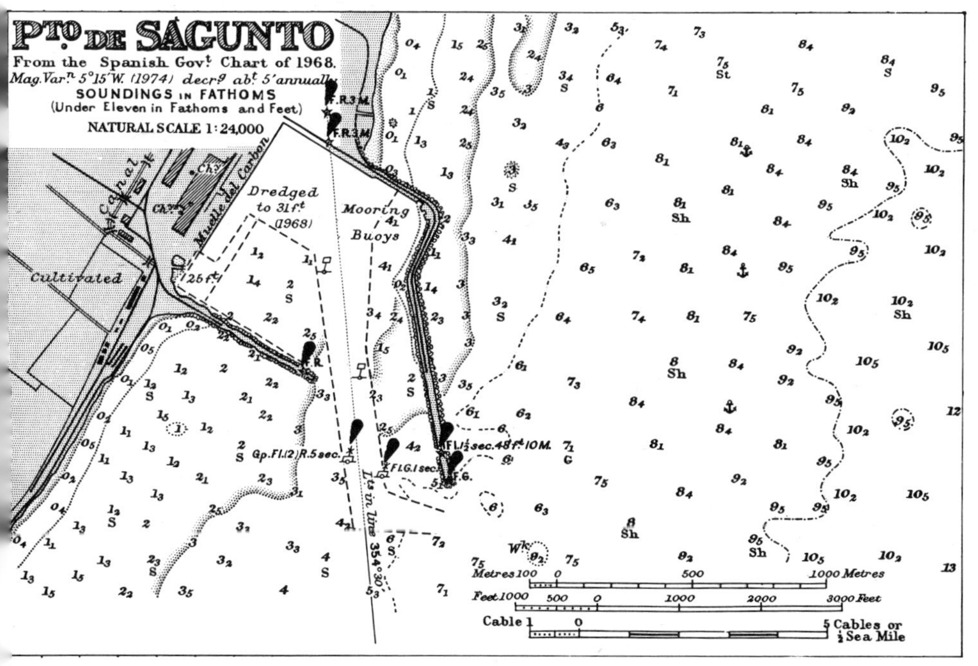

Valencia

Admiralty Chart 562   (pop: 625 000)

A beautiful city, third largest in Spain, situated 3k from the harbour where you will be made welcome at the hospitable Real Club Nautico.

Keep your eye open for shipping as you come round the mole and make for the entrance, on your left, towards the yacht club.

You will be made welcome here and there is every facility including a large open-air swimming pool. Palm trees overhang the pontoon, also the road outside the club but there is quite an extensive dock area to walk through on your way to the town.

Valencia with the masts of yachts showing the position of the Real Club Nautico.

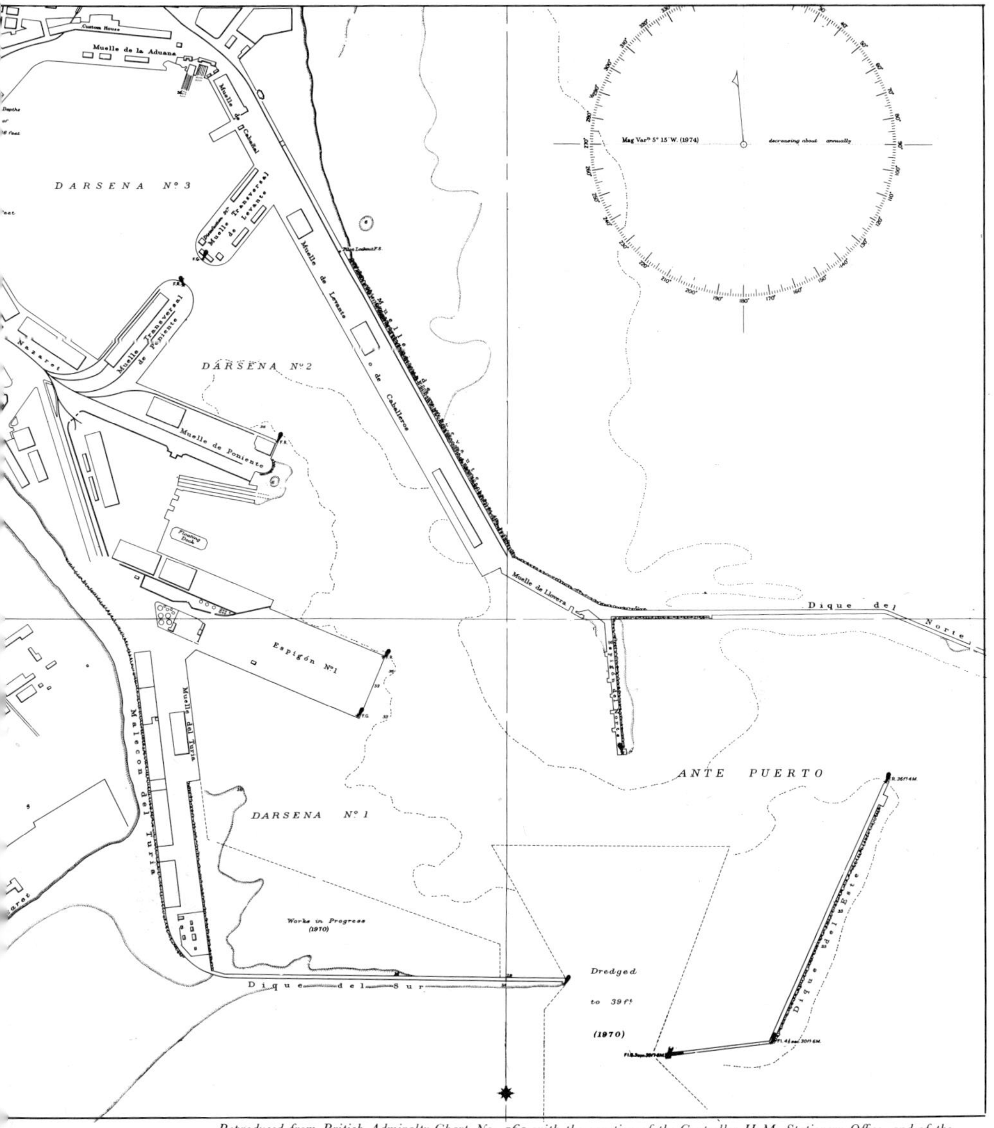

Reproduced from British Admiralty Chart No. 562 with the sanction of the Controller H.M. Stationery Office, and of the Hydrographer of the Navy.

Valencia Harbour.

There is a great deal of commercial activity in Valencia and quite a lot of tourism; it may strike you as being noisy and dusty and it will almost certainly be hot but the city has splendid shops and a sophisticated air.

In the centre of the city you will find the cathedral of interest; it has three portals, one Romanesque, one Gothic and one baroque. Inside there are paintings by Goya and Jacomart, goldsmith's work by Cellini and a chalice said to be the Holy Grail used by Jesus at the Last Supper. Other items of interest are the Basilica of La Virgen de los Desamparados; the Almudin, a medieval granary, now the Paleontological Museum and the Church of San Esteban where the Cid's daughters were married. Museums: the Provincial Museum of Fine Arts with Hieronymus Bosch, Van Dyck, Goya and a self-portrait of Velazquez; Colegio de Patriarcas with el Greco, Van der Weyden. The National Ceramics Museum; Provincial Anthropological Museum; Historical Museum.

FIESTAS: On 19 March the fiesta of San Jose begins when thousands of pounds worth of carnival figures go up in smoke and

Valencia harbour from the balcony of the Real Club Nautico.

The Real Club Nautico at Valencia has a fine swimming pool beside the harbour.

nobody sleeps for a week.

From the 20 to the 31 July is the July Fair with concerts, firework displays, ending with the famous battle of the flowers. During this fiesta, on St. James's Day, (25 July), there occurs one of the big bullfighting occasions when the best bullfighters of the season usually appear, (described, you may remember, by Hemingway in *Death in the afternoon*).

Whilst in Valencia do not forget that it is here that you are supposed to get the real, genuine *paella*.

Cullera

Admiralty Chart 1458   (pop: 16 000)

Cullera is a little way up the River Jucar, the entrance to which, from the sea, is between two moles.

Keep you echo-sounder going because it looks just the place to run aground; but all sorts and sizes of boats are tied up at Cullera, admittedly with the benefit of local knowledge.

You can tie up near shops but Cullera is mainly a tourist resort. The church you see dominating the surroundings is modern, the Virgen del Castillo, and is the object of pilgrimage.

The River Jucar at Cullera.

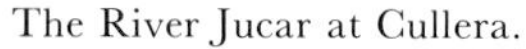

Gandia

Admiralty Chart 1320 (pop: 22 000)

The first thing you see on your left coming in is the ship-breaker's yard, not the most decorative welcome it must be admitted; unfortunately it sets the tone for the rest of the unattractive port area.

There is quite a small Club Nautico on your right coming in and, by it, a small quay.

In the port area are a few shops; the town of Gandia is 4k away and is quite a pleasant little town nestling under the Sierra de Gandia. In the 16thC it was the capital of a duchy ruled by the Borgias. The Ducal Palace is amongst places of interest; also the Santa Clara convent.

Gandia.

Reproduced from British Admiralty Chart No. 1320 with the sanction of the Controller H.M. Stationery Office, and of the Hydrographer of the Navy.

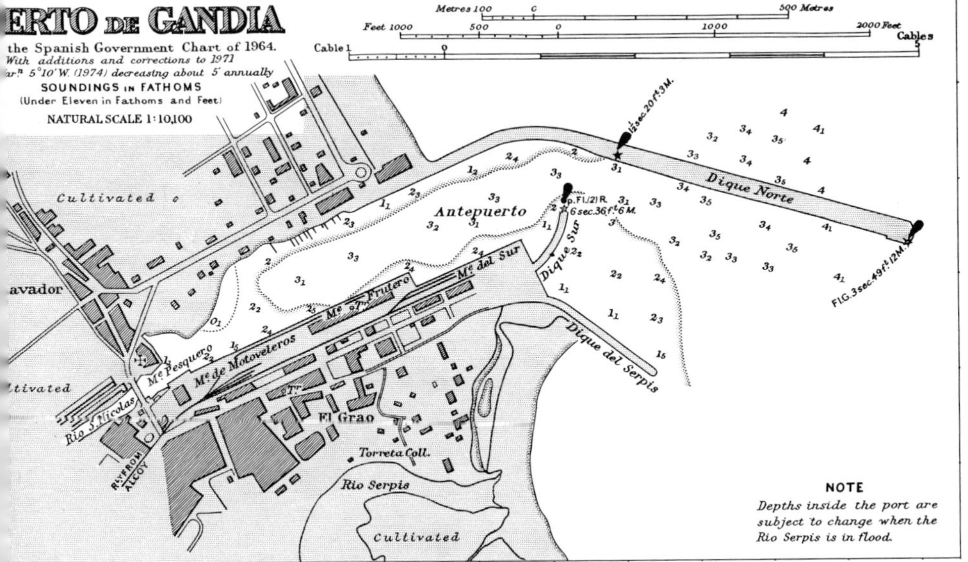

9 Costa Blanca

Distances between Harbours

	from Gandia	*Kms*
Denia		25
Javea		10
Calpe		25
Altea		7
Alicante		37
Santa Pola		15
Torrevieja		28
Portman		49
Escombrera		10
Cartagena		10
Mazarron		28
Aguilas		28
Garrucha		35
	Almeria	80

Average temperatures:

	Jan	Feb	Mar	Apl	May	Jun	Jly	Aug	Sep	Oct	Nov	Dec
MAX	61	63	68	72	78	84	90	90	86	77	70	63
MIN	44	43	47	50	56	61	66	68	65	59	50	45

Costa Blanca.

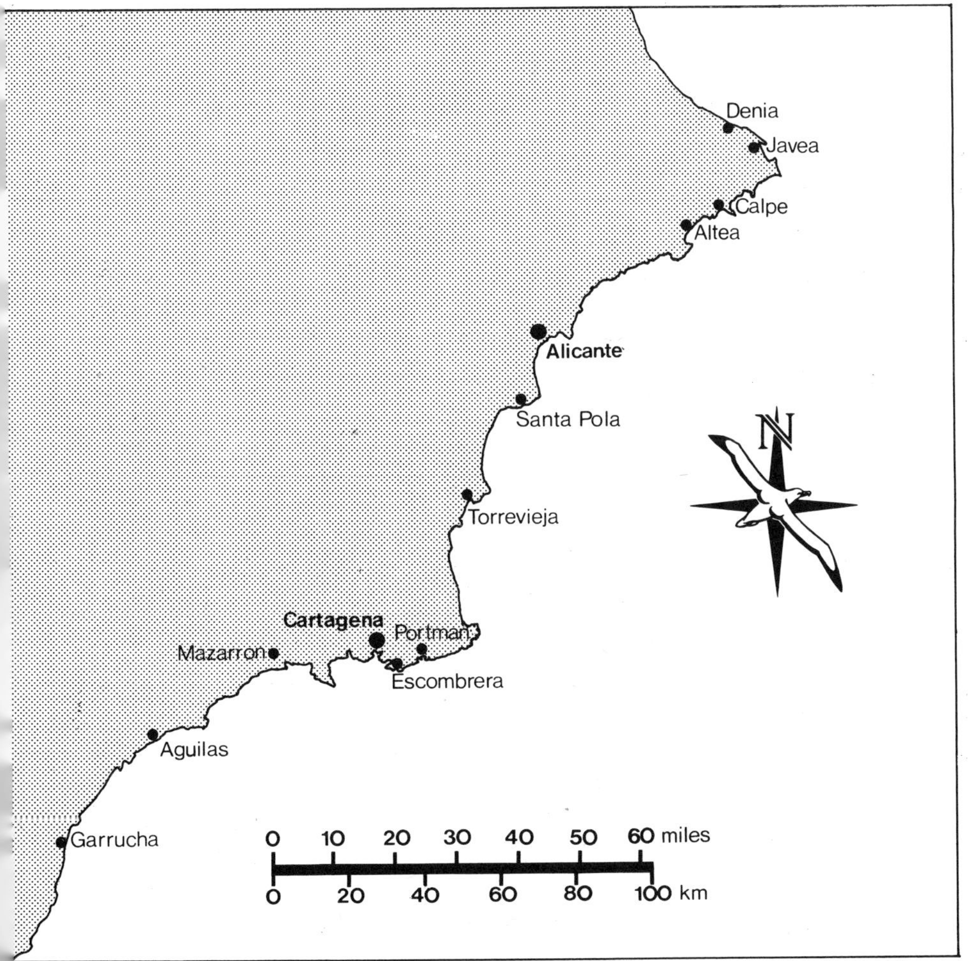

The Costa Blanca comprises two wide semi-circles or bays which meet and jut out to sea at Cape Palos.

Round the Cape de la Nao to the Costa Blanca and the summer temperatures start hitting the nineties for this coast is much hotter than the Costa Brava or the Costa del Sol. You can really start looking for a harbour to winter in from now on, a place where you will see the almond blossom in January. There are reputed to be less than twenty-five days of bad weather here in a year and the average number of days of sunshine a year is over three hundred.

The Costa Blanca receives its biggest load of holidaymakers in July and August and the weather is also really hot then so that you should organise your cruise schedule to visit this coast outside of the peak summer months.

It is an ideal coast for cruising although, later on, you will see that it has its industrial areas. For most of the time you will have sunshine, a cloudless deep blue sky, clear blue seas and an interesting variety of harbours. Ashore, on the coast and behind, there is also much of interest to see.

There are a number of harbours on this coast where you can winter in warmth inexpensively and many people do.

Alicante is a comparatively small port, and a pleasant one for yachtsmen, on an ideal coast for cruising.

Denia

Admiralty Chart 1458   (pop: 10 000)

A pleasant harbour, pleasant yacht club and a pleasant little town. Fishing boats are in a separate part of the harbour.

On entry you will see the new Club Nautico ahead of you with the slips to the right of it and pontoon moorings in front. Although it appears to be a small yachting harbour there are quays for vessels drawing up to 3m; it is, in fact, quite an important centre for the export of oranges.

The harbour and Club Nautico are near to the pleasant little town where you will find a good selection of shops, including a yacht chandlers.

As you pass the pavement coffee tables it seems that you hear the English language spoken more than any other for Denia is popular with British expatriates whose neat villas you see lining the hills as you come in.

The city, Greek in origin, once possessed a great temple of Diana, thus its name.

Denia is the terminal of the narrow gauge railway to Alicante.

Denia, showing the Club Nautico on the left.

TRUE NORTH
Placer de la Placeta
Dique Norte
Dique Sur
El Caballo
Gp.Fl.(3)G.
Ldg. in line 228°
La Androna
Gp.Fl.(2)R.
Fl.G.
Fl.G.
Fl.G.
Bajo Guitarro
Pillar
El Blancar
Magnetic Pillar
Pta del Raset
Slipway
Dénia Castle
286
Church T.
DENIA
(Lifeboat)
(Pilots)
Sta Antonio Ch.
Steam Saw Mill
Bull Ring
F.R.33ft.7M.
F.R.46ft.7M.
Slipway
Mooring Piles
Placer de San Nicolás
Escollo de S.Nicolás
Rincón de San Nicolás
Pta del Barranquet
Pta de la Sota
Pta de S. Nicolás
Cemetery
Chalet
PTO. DE DÉNIA
Dénia Castle ⊙ Lat.38°50'30"N.. Long 0°6'29"E.
Natural Scale 1: 18,210
Mag.Varn. 5°55'W.(1964) decreasing about 7' annually
52'
52'
38° 51'
38° 51'
50'
50'

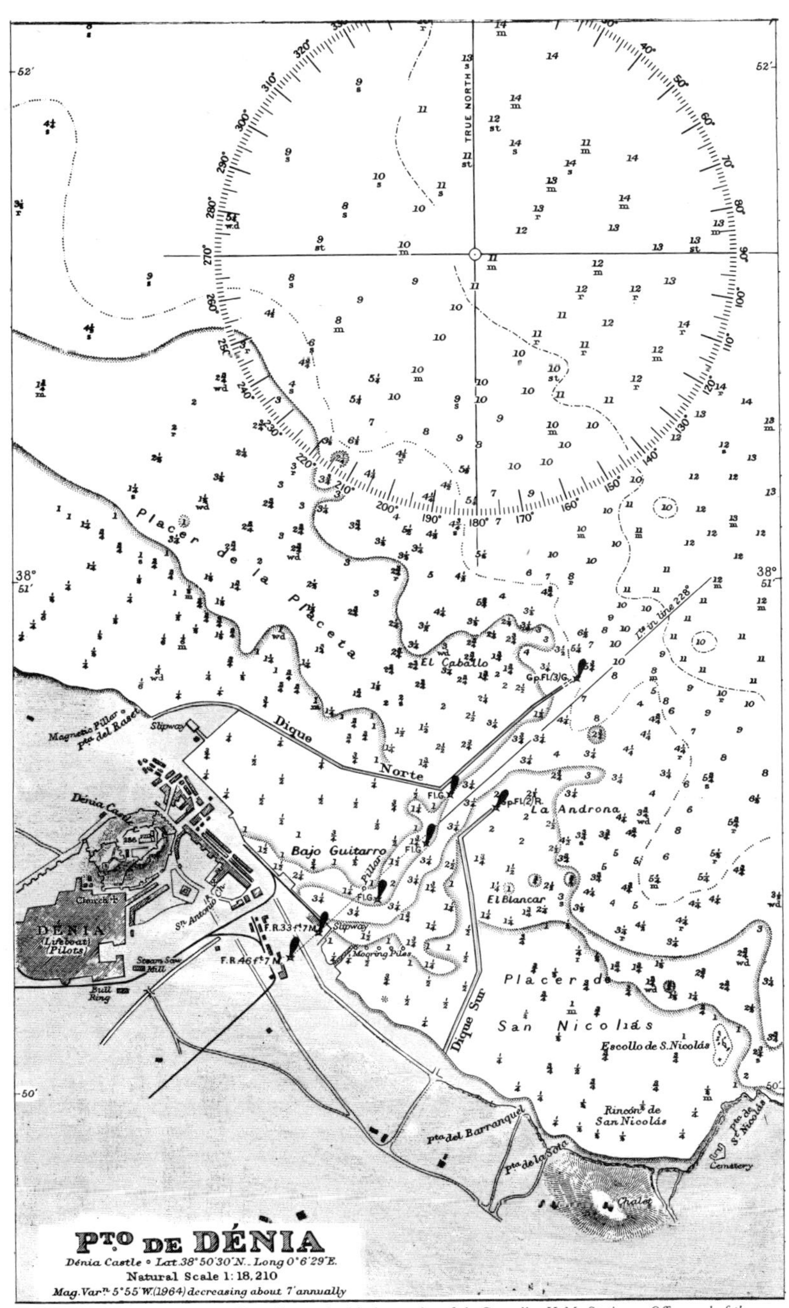

Denia.

Javea

Admiralty Chart 1187   (pop: 6000)

This is a splendid little yacht harbour with an excellent
Club Nautico. By now, with your experience of Spanish harbours
you will not be going in too close to quay walls without keeping
a careful eye on what lies below the surface of that translucent
water; Javea is no exception.

From a harbour point of view Javea is almost perfect but
there is not much of interest ashore; a pleasant enough village
with shops that sell all your daily needs, certainly, but it is rather
remote from civilization. You may consider this an advantage of
course. There are no fishing boats in this harbour.

If you are trying to get away from it all, Javea is the place
for you. On, or under, Cape San Antonio there are many
grottoes, some of them only accessible from the sea; there are in
them stalactites and also a small freshwater lake in the Tallada
cave.

There are always a number of cruising yachts in this
harbour.

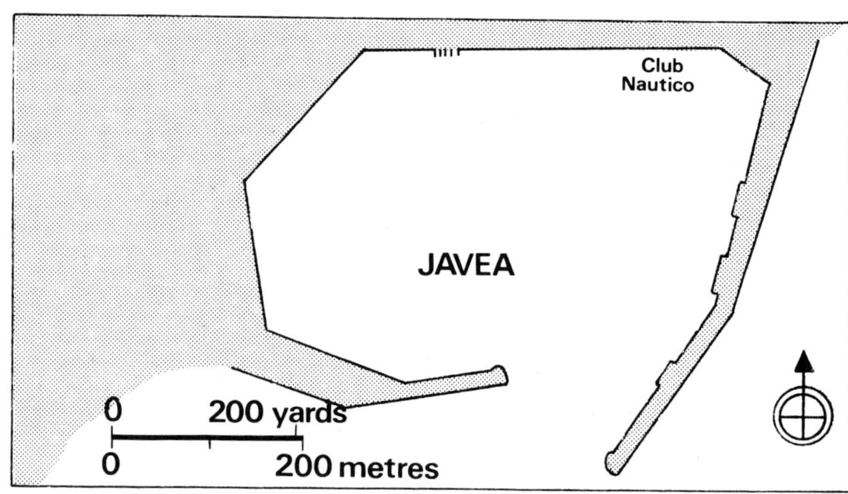

Javea with the Club Nautico on the left.

The public quay of
Javea with the club
moorings behind.

The yacht yard with its slip is the white building, but Calpe is not really
recommended for the cruising yacht except in emergency.

Calpe

Admiralty Chart 1372   (pop: 3000)

Mainly a fishing boat harbour, in fact when the fleet returns in the evenings there are so many fishing boats churning into the harbour that a visiting yacht feels like an interloper.

Calpe is not really recommended for a cruising yacht except in an emergency; but there is a yacht yard there, or rather a Navale Constructionnes where large fishing boats are built—and usually there are two or three yachts on the slip for repairs.

Calpe lies under a 1000ft high rock, the Penon de Ifach, sometimes likened to the Rock of Gibraltar. You can go up inside this rock to the top and look back for miles along the coast you have cruised along and ahead at the coast awaiting you.

Ashore Calpe has nothing of interest for the yachtsman. There are no shops near the harbour, but there is an evening fish auction. The village shops are a long walk away. All around are the villas of the British, German, Belgian expatriates; monstrous tower blocks of flats seem to suffocate what was quite an undistinguished village to start with. Much of the time there are coaches alongside, spilling out pink package-holidaymakers from Benidorm.

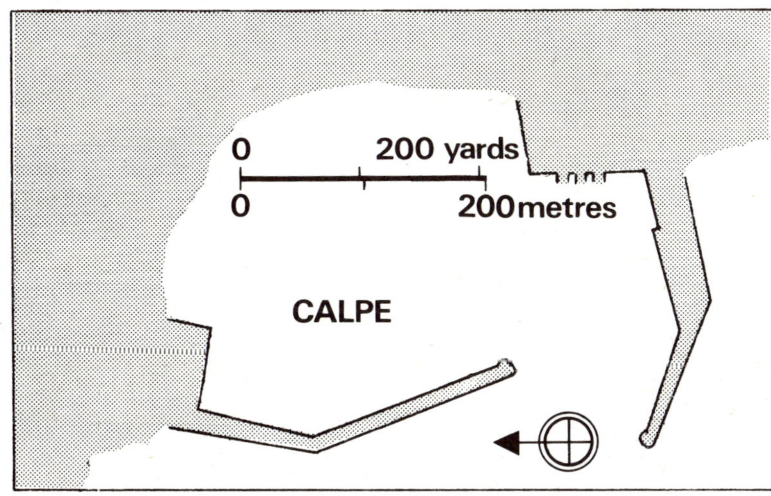

Altea

Admiralty Chart 1372   (pop: 7000)

The harbour is formed by two moles and yachts anchor in the middle, also towards the yacht building yard which will be seen over towards your right as you enter the harbour.

Ashore there is a good selection of shops, on the other side of the busy main road but within easy walking distance. There is also an interesting market but this seems to be changing its character to cater for the increasing coach-loads of holidaymakers.

Sheltered to the north by the Sierra Bernia, 3715ft, and to the south by the Sierra Helada, 1395ft, an attractive bay, four miles across, is formed.

The yacht building yard in Altea is on the right.

Alicante

Admiralty Charts 469, 1372   (pop: 150 000)

As you approach Alicante you see above it, on your right, the vast Moorish castle of Santa Barbara; rounding the mole you pass across the outer commercial harbour and turn in to the inner harbour, proceeding to where you see yachts lying on the quay wall, anchored and by the Club Nautico. Secure here, usually stern-to.

Alicante is a comparatively small port and a pleasant one; from here wine, olives, raisins etc., are exported and ships leave regularly for the Balearics, Marseilles, Oran.

Ashore the palm shaded avenues are supposed to be unique in that the fruit on the trees actually ripens. Alicante is so attractive to the yachtsman because the climate is so perfect, because the harbour is so near to such a gay and attractive town, because the finest sandy beaches are so near; but because of all these attractions it is too popular with yachts and crowded a lot of the time. Some time ago there was a clear out of what one might describe as yachting bums but, needless to say, no reader

Entering Alicante approach the white building on the seafront to the left.

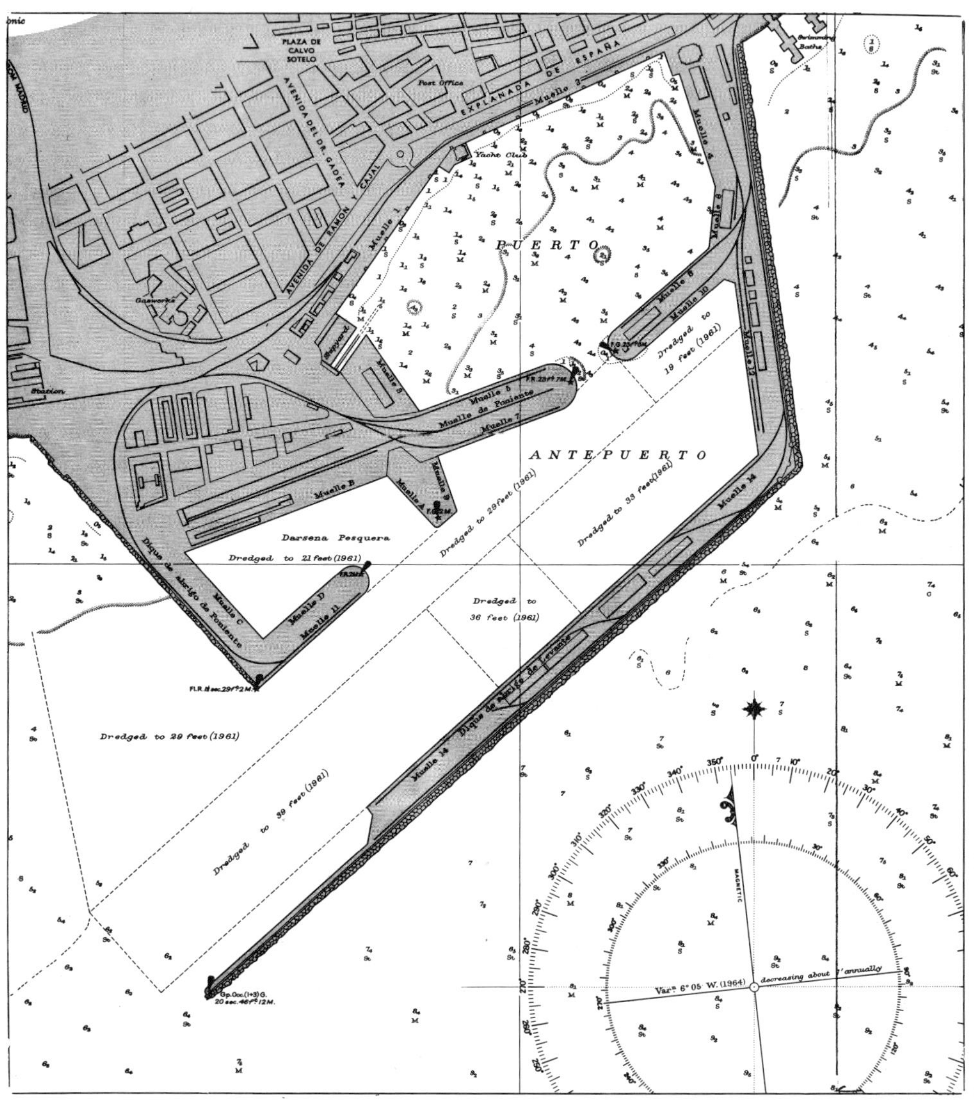

Alicante.

Reproduced from British Admiralty Chart No. 469 with the sanction of the Controller H.M. Stationery Office, and of the Hydrographer of the Navy.

of this book would fit into this category.

Many cruising yachtsmen speak of Alicante as the perfect harbour. You must make a point of visiting it and it is likely that you will want to stay there for as long as you can.

The town is attractive and yet not besieged by tourists. Of interest is the Baroque city hall, Parish church of Santa Maria, Cathedral of San Nicolas, 18thC, a fascinating market, museums, a race course and, of course, a bullring. The Santa Barbara Castle mentioned earlier can be visited by a lift that 'scales' the heights of Cerro Benacantil.

The nearby Tarbarca Island may tempt you to cruise 10k to see its old fortifications or to search for its hidden treasure.

The June Fiesta is something to experience, lasting from the 21st to the 30th and including the famous bonfires of San Juan.

Only twenty-six miles away is the famous palm forest of Elche, the only one in Europe.

Alicante may be crowded in the summer.

Santa Pola

Admiralty Chart 1372   (pop: 9000)

Rounding the mole you see the fishing boats lying on the quay to your right. You can secure beyond them, alongside or at anchor where convenient in the harbour.

Santo Pola is mainly a fishing boat harbour. The small town is quite attractive and there are some shops near to the harbour.

In Santa Pola secure by the fishing boats.

Torrevieja

Admiralty Charts 1458, 1372 (pop: 10 000)

This is a large harbour with small marina-type moorings by the Club Nautico; they are immediately in view upon entering the harbour.

The town though small is quite an important tourist centre, noted principally for the Summer Festival of Habanera for musical and choral groups.

Torrevieja.

Reproduced from British Admiralty Chart No. 1544 with the sanction of the Controller H.M. Stationery Office, and of the Hydrographer of the Navy.

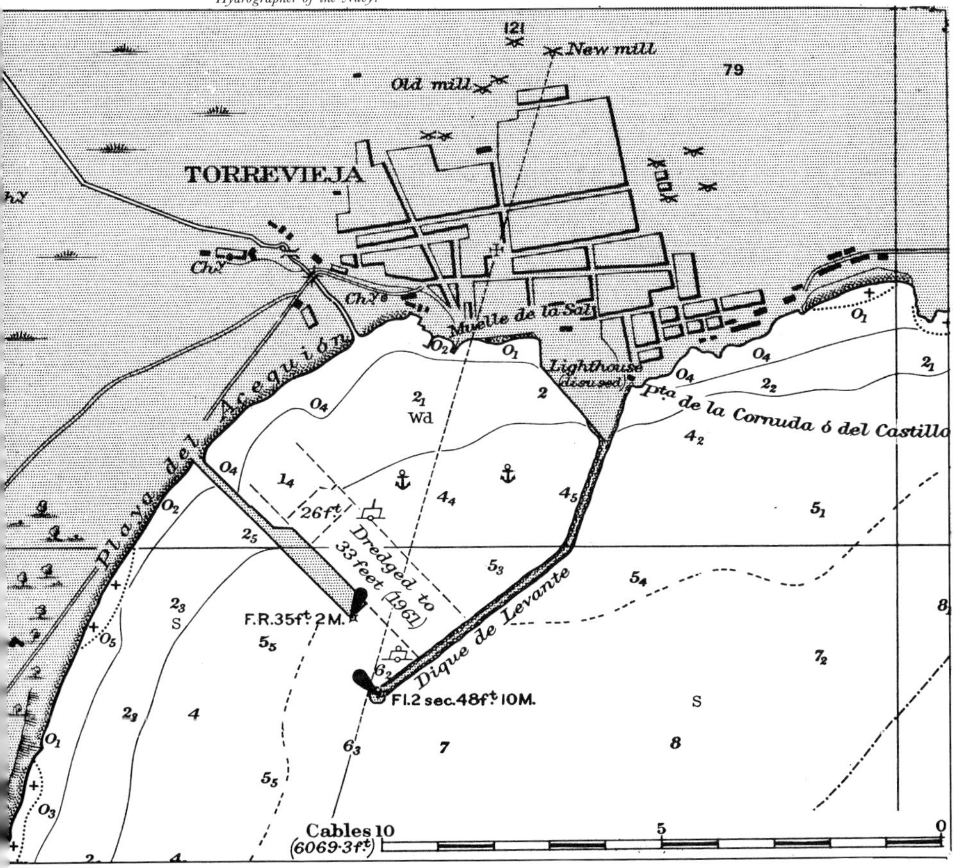

Torrevieja harbour from the breakwater.

There are shops catering for most needs within walking distance of the harbour.

Next along the coast is the Mar Menor, included because it will excite your curiosity when you see what appear to be buildings in the middle of the sea. They are on the San Pedro reef, a strip 16 miles long that helps to enclose the Mar Menor, (little sea).

There is a shallow break in the reef but much obstructed by sandbanks, also a small harbour for the use of Spanish naval aircraft.

The mainland of the Mar Menor is being developed as a multi-million pound holiday resort and the scheme will include 'houseboat-cruisers' in the lagoon.

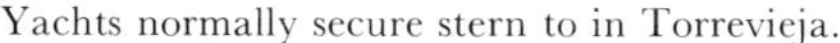

Yachts normally secure stern to in Torrevieja.

Portman

Admiralty Chart 2717

Seeking information as we do, my wife and I have been into some unattractive places but we nearly jibbed at Portman. With nothing to see as you approach except ore mines and petrol refineries it is at first sight, (and subsequent sights), a hilly area of the most hideous industrial spoliation.

Silting up across the bay has recently been reported, so great care and attention to the echo sounder should be exercised on approach.

Portman.

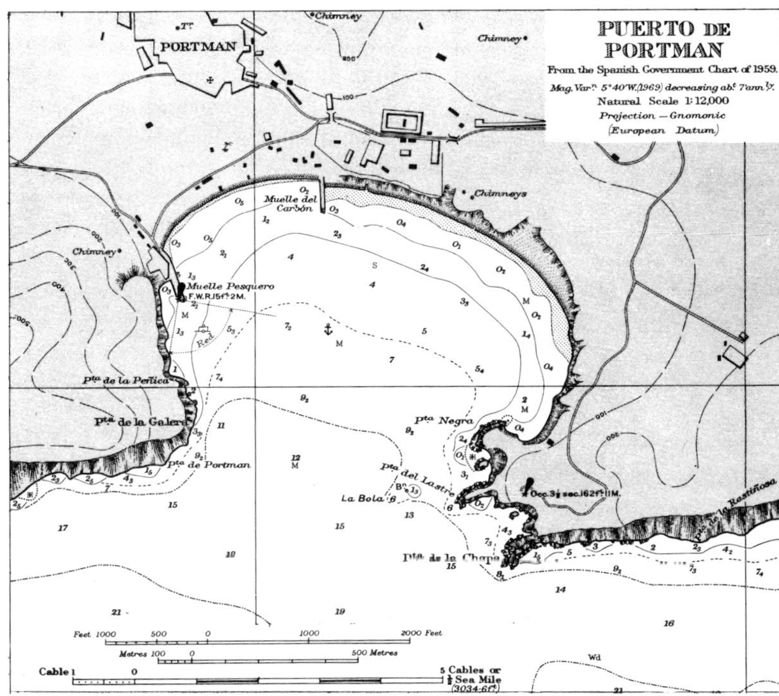

Escombrera

Admiralty Chart 1194

This is still an area of heavy industry. Countries must have these shoreside horrors, (think of our beautiful Solent!).

Escombrera is now almost exclusively a tanker harbour, and is of little interest to the cruising yacht.

Escombrera and (*right*) Cartagena.

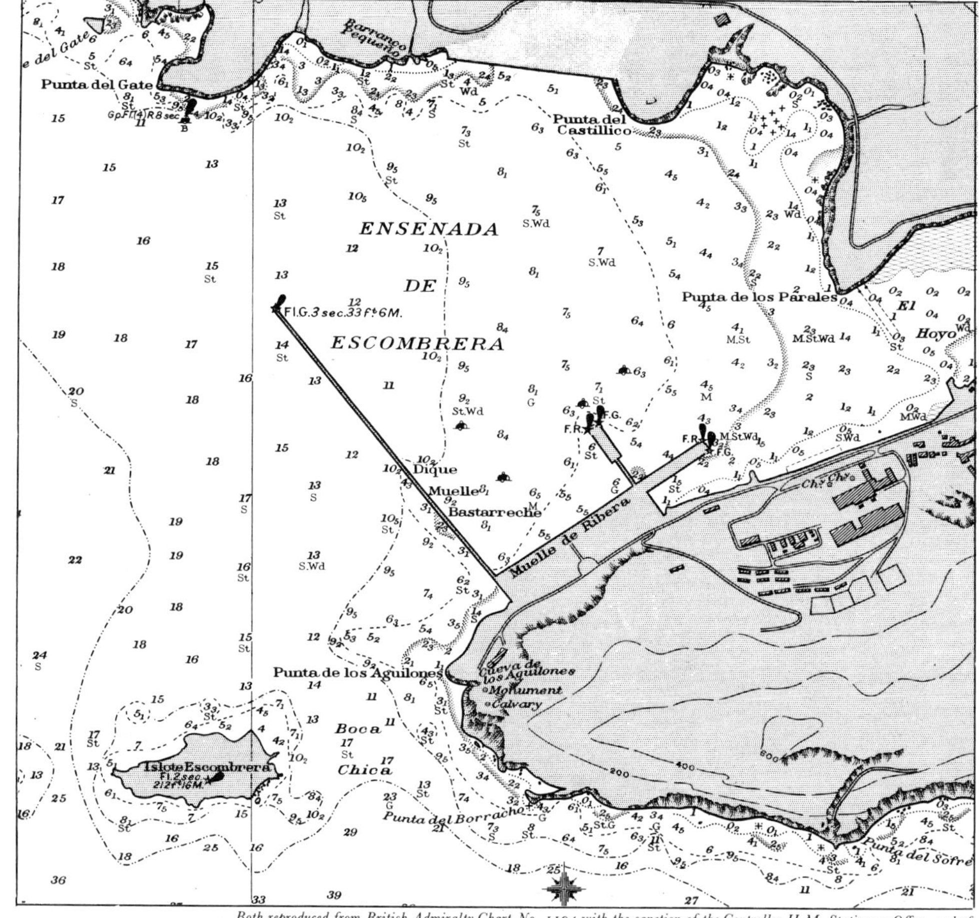

Both reproduced from British Admiralty Chart No. 1194 with the sanction of the Controller H.M. Stationery Office, and of the Hydrographer of the Navy.

Cartagena

Admiralty Chart 1194   (pop: 150 000)

You will see the ruined castles as you approach, guarding this almost land-locked bay; you are sure to see a warship moored stern-to and therefore facing you ahead. To the left of it you will see yachts at the small jetty by the Club Nautico.

The town is within easy walking distance of the harbour and there are shops of all descriptions.

Cartagena is a naval base, headquarters of the Spanish Naval Command with an arsenal and shipyards, also it is a big cargo port.

From here Hannibal set out for Italy in 218 BC. In this harbour sailors mutinied at the 1936 Nationalist rising and the warships remained Republican; in 1939 they mutinied again and the warships were sent to French Tunisia to be interned.

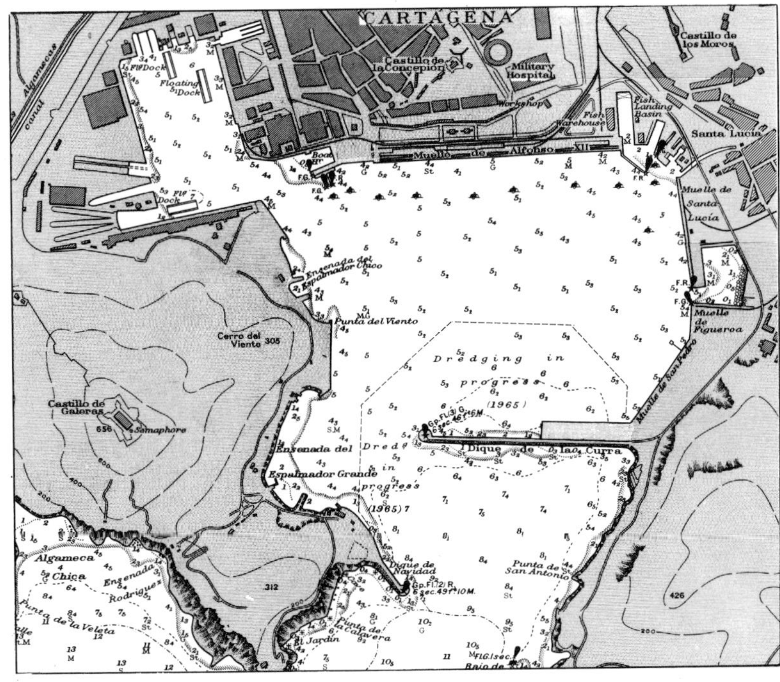

Mazarron

Admiralty Chart 2717   (pop: 10 000)

This is an excellent shelter from westerly winds but, apart from this, is of no interest to the yachtsman.

Ashore all is shoddiness extending inland as far as the eye can see, Mazarron being a centre of the iron ore industry.

Mazarron.   *Reproduced from British Admiralty Chart No. 1544 with the sanction of the Controller H.M. Stationery Office, and of the Hydrographer of the Navy.*

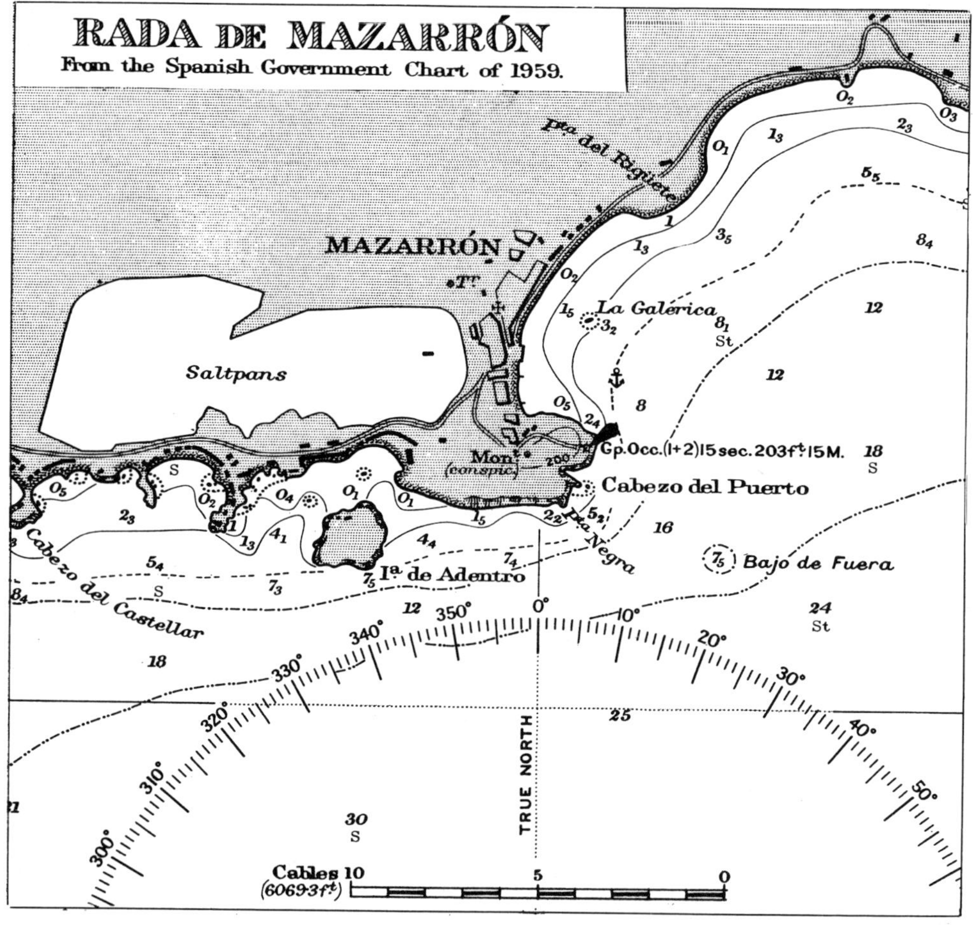

Aguilas

Admiralty Chart 2717

(pop: 17 000)

This is a pleasant little harbour; the castle on the left as you come in is your guide. Look for the quay on your left and prepare to moor stern-to.

There is some tourism here but it does not intrude. The shops are within walking distance and you can get most things that you are likely to need.

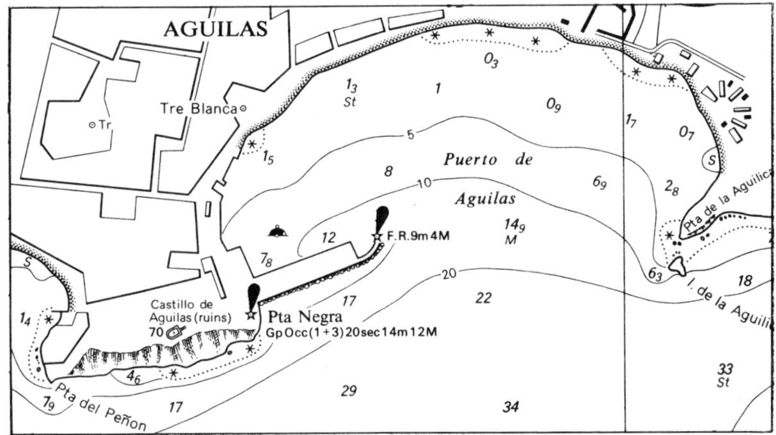

Reproduced from British Admiralty Chart No. 1588 with the sanction of the Controller H.M. Stationery Office, and of the Hydrographer of the Navy.

Aguilas has a pleasant little harbour.

Garrucha

Admiralty Chart 774   (pop: 3500)

A small harbour, principally a fishing village but with some shipping for there are foundries and iron ore mines here; needless to say they do not add to the attractions ashore.

A small Club Nautico caters for small craft and shops are available nearby.

Looking out to the entrance of Garrucha harbour.

Inside the harbour at Garrucha.

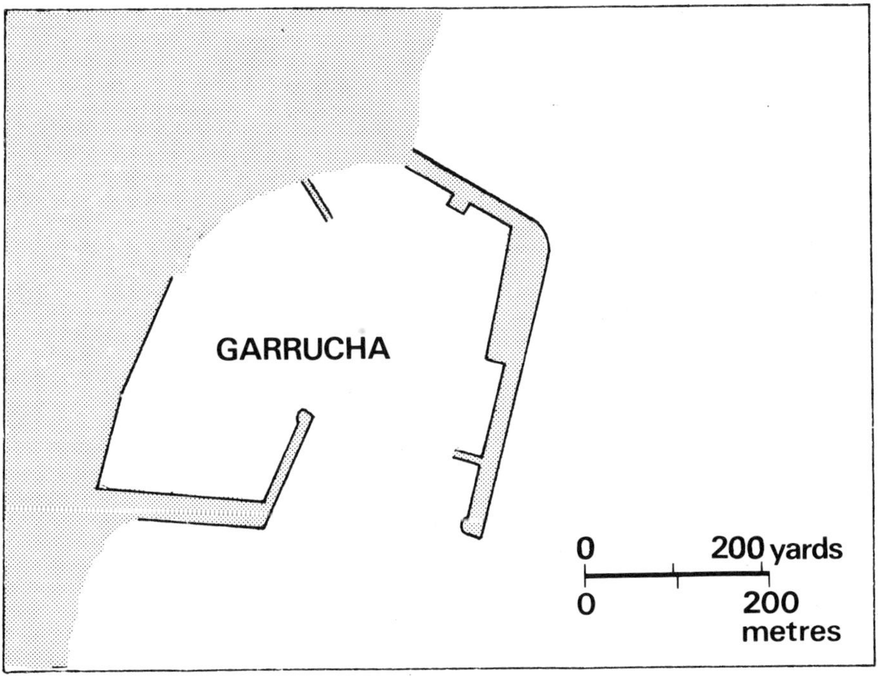

10 Costa Del Sol

Distances between Harbours

from Garrucha	Kms
Almeria	80
Adra	49
Motril	43
Almunecar	15
Malaga	54
Fuengirola	26
Marbella	25
Jose Banus	6
Estepona	24
Gibraltar	35

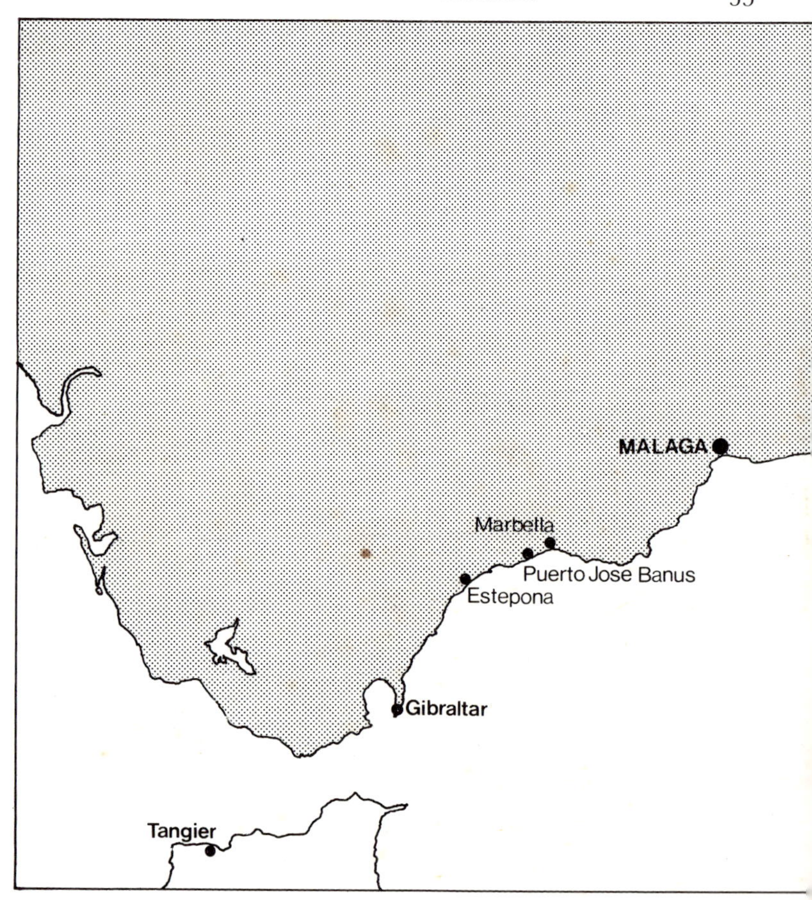

The Costa del Sol is our last section of the mainland coast; it takes in practically the entire Mediterranean coast of Andalusia. The 'foreign' yachts that you see this far down are usually on their purposeful way to the Canaries in preparation for the further consideration of an Atlantic crossing.

There are rather lengthy stretches between some of the harbours on this section of coast but there are some good harbours for yachts and a winter climate to tempt you to stay in them.

Ashore some of the coastline has been transformed in comparatively recent years by the development of chrome and concrete hotels overlooking turquoise coloured bathing pools but there are also the natural contrasting colours of trees and shrubs, whitewashed houses set amidst flowers and cactus.

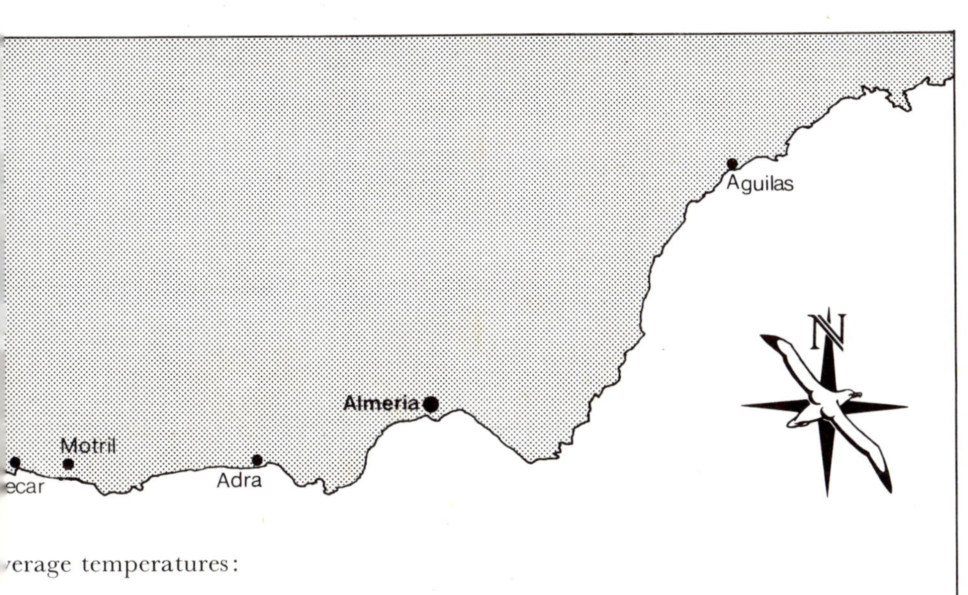

verage temperatures:

	Jan	Feb	Mar	Apl	May	Jun	Jly	Aug	Sep	Oct	Nov	Dec
AX	63	63	67	70	74	81	84	86	84	74	68	63
IN	49	49	52	56	59	66	70	72	68	61	54	49

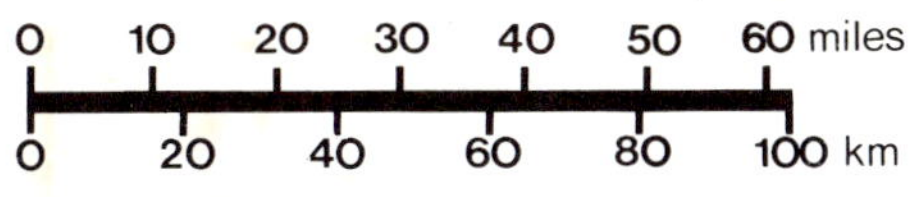

Almeria

Admiralty Chart 1588   (pop: 90 000)

This is a big commercial harbour but it is quite pleasant and unspoiled.

On entry you will be able to distinguish between the cargo wharves and the yacht moorings without difficulty; on proceeding towards the moored yachts you will see the Club Nautico.

From the Club Nautico a palm-tree lined road leads to the main street with stylish shops, marble pavements, chromium plated news kiosks and pavement-cafe-glasshouses as in Paris and elsewhere.

Everything you are likely to require is within a short walking distance of the harbour.

There is a 16thC Cathedral; the ruin of the Moorish castle, the Alcazaba, decorated with a Gothic tower, 15thC; the castle of San Cristobal with a chapel built by the Knights Templar, 12thC.

Almeria.   *Reproduced from British Admiralty Chart No. 1588 with the sanction of the Controller H.M. Stationery Office, and of the Hydrographer of the Navy.*

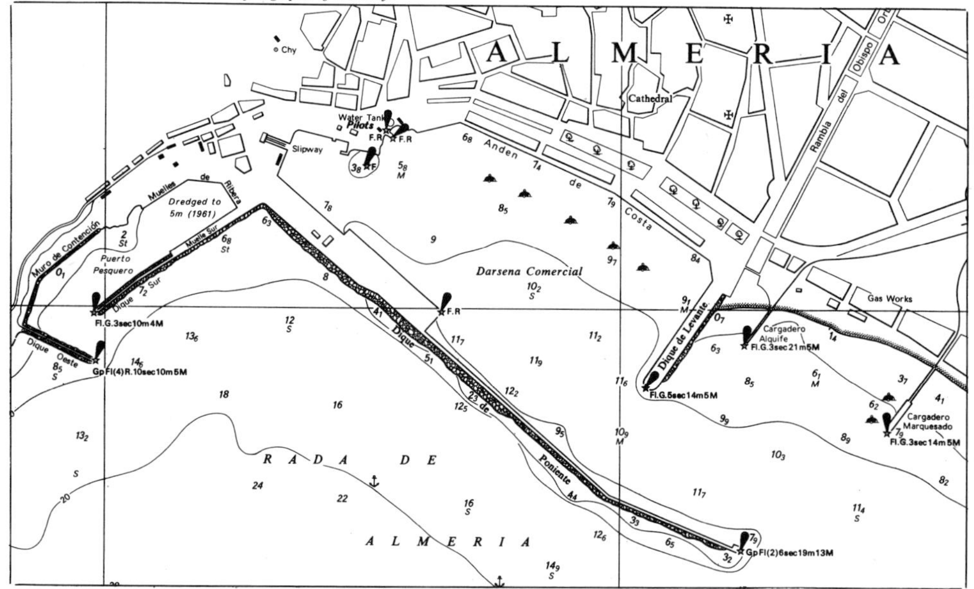

The Cathedral, Almeria.

Adra

Admiralty Chart 2717   (pop: 16 000)

The harbour is formed by two moles and you could take shelter here from northerly and easterly winds.

It is mainly a fishing boat harbour; over by the chimney in the corner you will see boats being built and hauled out for repair, also the small *lamparas* close in to the shore.

As always, watch your echo sounder and be ready to let go; if you tie up on the quay you will find yourself in the middle of a fishing industry that seems to work around the clock.

The old town is situated at the foot of a hill, on the River Adra, and produces fruit and also some fine fish.

There are shops within convenient distance of the harbour.

Adra—proceed towards the big chimney.

Torre de Perdigones
PUERTO DE ADRA
From the Spanish Government Chart of 1960.
With additions and corrections to 1966.
Dique de Poniente Light _ Lat. 36°44' 33".9 N, Long. 3°01'05".1 W.(approx.)
(European Datum)
Mag. Var.n 6°30'W. (1969) decreasing about 7' annually.
Cultivated
Muelle y Dique de Poniente
G
St
St
St
St
St
St
Fl.G. 5 sec. 30ft. 4M.
Gp.Fl.(2)R.6 sec. 28ft. 3M.
Metres 100   0   500 Metres
Feet 1000   500   0   1000   2000 Feet

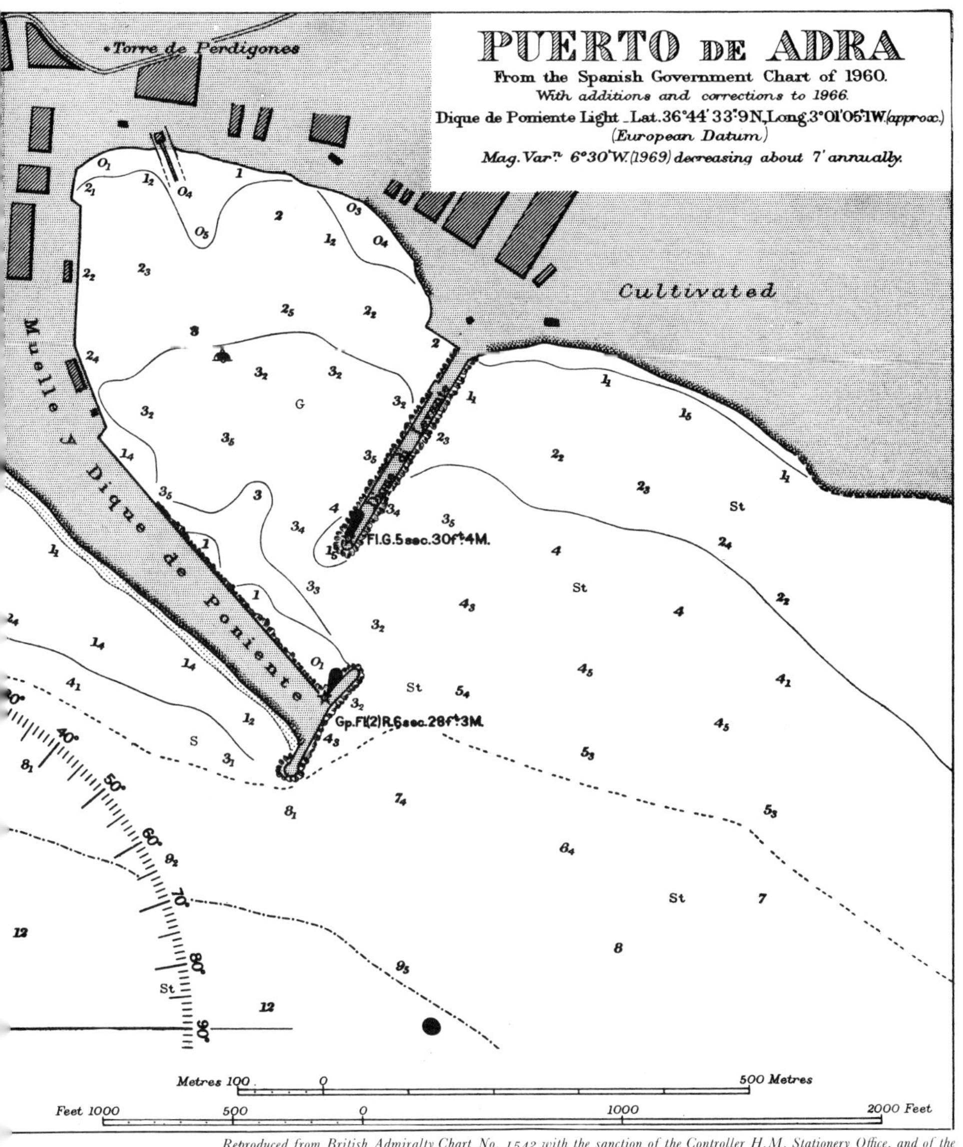

dra.

Motril

Admiralty Charts 773, 2717   (pop: 30 000)

The port of Motril is protected by two moles; it is a commercial and fishing boat harbour. There is no problem in finding a mooring on the quay by the club or anchor opposite, but, unfortunately, the shore amenities are somewhat shabby. Odd shops are near to the harbour but the town of Motril is over a mile away from your mooring, past sugar cane fields and tramping lines of load-bearing donkeys.

The town of Motril, centre of the sugar-cane country, was once a Moorish stronghold and the white, cube shaped Moorish type houses against a rich background of flowers is attractive.

There are all facilities at the friendly Yacht Club.

Places to Visit: Granada is only 70k from Motril by road or rail.

Motril.

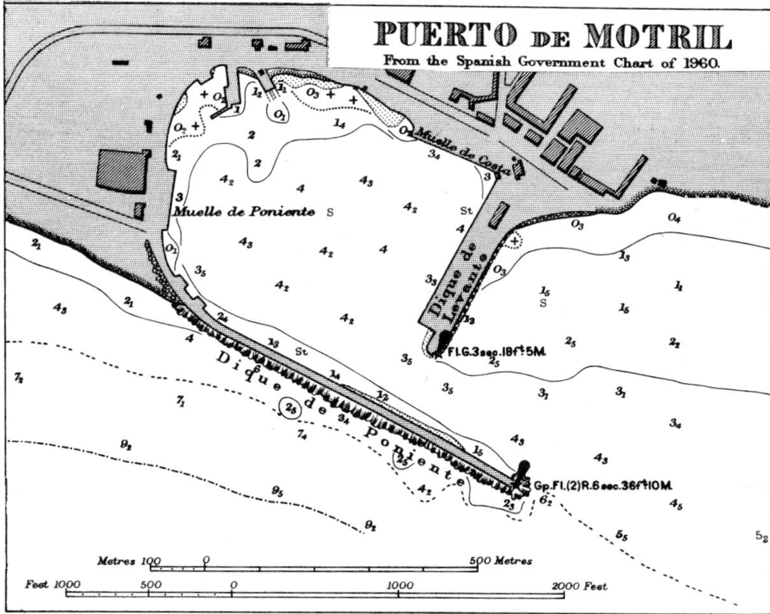

The port of Motril and the Spanish countryside nearby.

Almunecar

Admiralty Charts 773, 2717   (pop: 13 000)

A small fishing port with an attractive background of whitewashed houses built in tiers below the remains of a Moorish castle.

Because it is such a picturesque place, with flowers displayed on wrought iron balconies, it attracts the tourists who throng the steep narrow streets, the beach and the harbour.

There are no shops near to the harbour.

Places to Visit: NERJA, to see the coastline from the viewpoint known as the balcony of Europe and the Nerja caves, half a mile long and 200ft high.

Malaga harbour.

Reproduced from British Admiralty Chart No. 1848 with the sanction of the Controller H.M. Stationery Office, and of the Hydrographer of the Navy.

Malaga

Admiralty Charts 1848, 773   (pop: 300 000)

Two moles protect Malaga harbour and from near the root of each another mole extends, forming an inner harbour. It is a deep water port for ocean liners but you will see the yacht moorings to your right as you enter. You will get the impression that the Club Nautico does not cater for yachts.

Malaga is an attractive town with shops of every description, some shopping areas being quite elegant and sophisticated. There are tree lined streets, sub-tropical shrubs, lovely parks and gardens as befits the capital of the Costa del Sol; there is also the old town with shabby alleyways.

You should visit the fruit, vegetable and fish market along the Calle de Torre Gorda; the Alcabaza, ancient palace of the Arab kings of Malaga; the Archaeological Museum; the Cathedral, part 16thC; Gibralfaro Castle; Roman theatre; Episcopal Palace and the Fine Arts Museum—El Greco, Zurbaran etc.

Pablo Picasso was born here in 1881 and for a time he

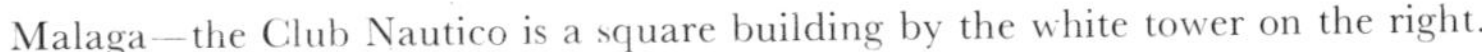

Malaga—the Club Nautico is a square building by the white tower on the right.

Malaga (*continued*)
taught in Malaga.

Across the bay is the Club Nautico el Candado, a very small harbour but able to accommodate quite large yachts.

Club Nautico el Candado is across the bay at Malaga . . .

. . . with a narrow entrance.

Fuengirola

Admiralty Chart 773   (pop: 18 000)

Recently developed and improved this is now quite a good harbour, though not at first easy to discern when you are standing off since it is set amidst four miles of beaches at the base of the Sierras de Mijas: but you see the ruins of the Sohail Castle and below it the marine promenade.

Secure on the quay by the yacht club or, if there is no room, by the mole opposite. There are all facilities here and a conveniently situated shopping centre.

Fuengirola is quite a centre for excursions to the Sierra Blanca.

Marbella

Admiralty Chart 1588   (pop: 15 000)

There is a small fishing boat and yacht harbour but adjacent to it is an ore transporter, or overhead ore conveyor and, of course, the proximity of this is not an attraction.

Marbella's prosperity depended upon its iron ore mines, (there are still blast furnaces), before the arrival of the tourist gold. Its splendid new hotels have an international clientele.

Anchor in the middle and enquire the moorings position at the Club Nautico. You will be made welcome here.

Most shops are available.

Marbella.

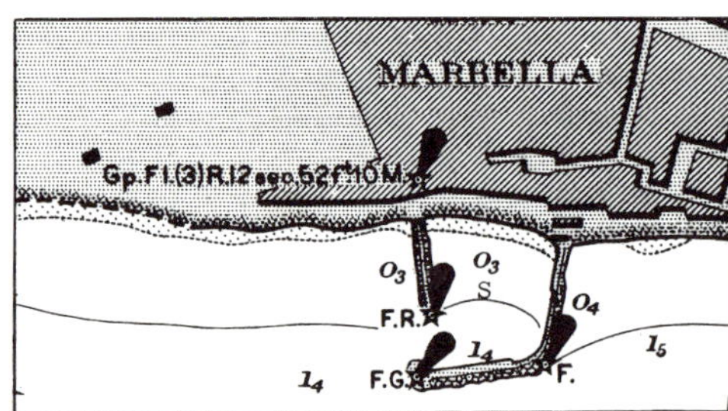

Reproduced from British Admiralty Chart No. 1542 with the sanction of the Controller H.M. Stationery Office, and of the Hydrographer of the Navy.

Marbella from the Club Nautico.

Puerto Jose Banus

There is no need to be on the look-out for commercial traffic or fishing boats when you round the mole of this harbour; neither need you take any avoiding action when you see a uniformed seaman in a boat approaching you for he is coming to bring you in. Unless, perhaps, it happens to be early in the morning and then the uniformed boatmen will be plucking offensive cigarette ends from the water, a daily task.

Once your boat is secure in her immaculate marina mooring you may wish to rest and sleep—in the hotel perhaps? Or you may prefer a modern chalet or a comfortable apartment? The beautiful little apartamento/bijou residences, Andalusia style that you see around the harbour by the administrative tower, (the 'Dock of Honour',) are sold, unfortunately; in fact the day that

Puerto Jose Banus.

Puerto Jose Banus expects 320 days of sunshine each year and has an immaculate marina.

they were put on sale at twenty thousand or two hundred thousand or whatever, they were all snapped up.

When you are hungry the port restaurants are ready to serve you. When you feel like a little exercise you may prefer a round of golf on either of the two 18-hole golf courses, or riding, or tennis, or clay pigeon shooting?

Inaugurated in May 1970, the Jose Banus Marina is a 38-acre luxury harbour created from nothing except, of course, that the 320 days of sunshine and the Mediterranean were already there. A thousand metres of quays and a thousand metres of piers; depth of water from 3 to 7.50 metres; a 36-ton boat lift; 5-ton self-propelled crane, ramp, slipway, two fuel supply stations, plus direct fuel supply at some quays; electricity, pressurized water, nationally linked telephone, TV aerial connections and fire extinguishing system to each berth; a permanent guard service, repair workshops, service station and parking for cars, toilets, garbage collection, permanent cleaning service, laundries, boutiques . . . all you need is here.

In the nearby seaside village with its six hundred metres of artificial beach there are swimming pools, bars, restaurants plus restaurants, bars, fashion shops, night clubs, discotheques.

It is six kilometres from the town of Marbella.

This is a splendid and beautifully conceived harbour; but when I see the increasing so-called luxury facilities being provided at new marinas all over the world it seems to me that the boating connection is getting increasingly superfluous.

Estepona

Admiralty Chart 1588

A small port, somewhat occupied with fishing boats although there is a small Club Nautico and a quay where you can moor stern-to.

It is quite a good harbour a longish walk from the town, on either side of which are the rivers Monterroso and Cala Pacheco. You will see the bridges to the west of the town.

Estepona ends the 106-mile coastline of the Costa del Sol that began at Motril, and therefore ends our cruise down the Spanish mainland.

The next port of call is Gibraltar and there are difficulties with Spain here, in fact at the time of writing access to Gibraltar from any part of the Spanish mainland is impossible.

Estepona.

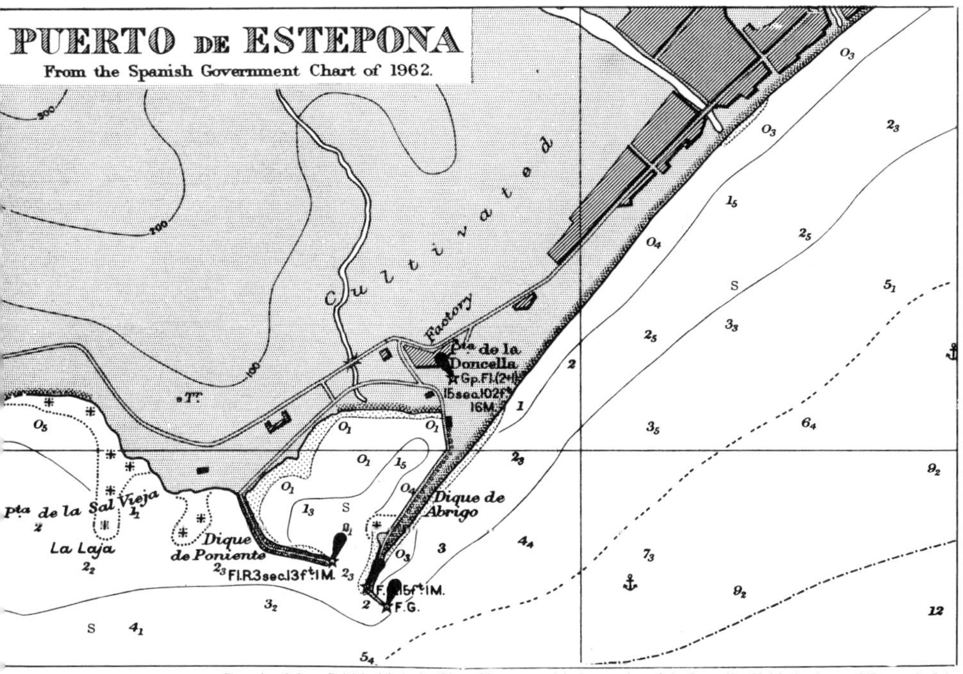

Reproduced from British Admiralty Chart No. 1542 with the sanction of the Controller H.M. Stationery Office, and of the Hydrographer of the Navy.

11 Balearic Islands

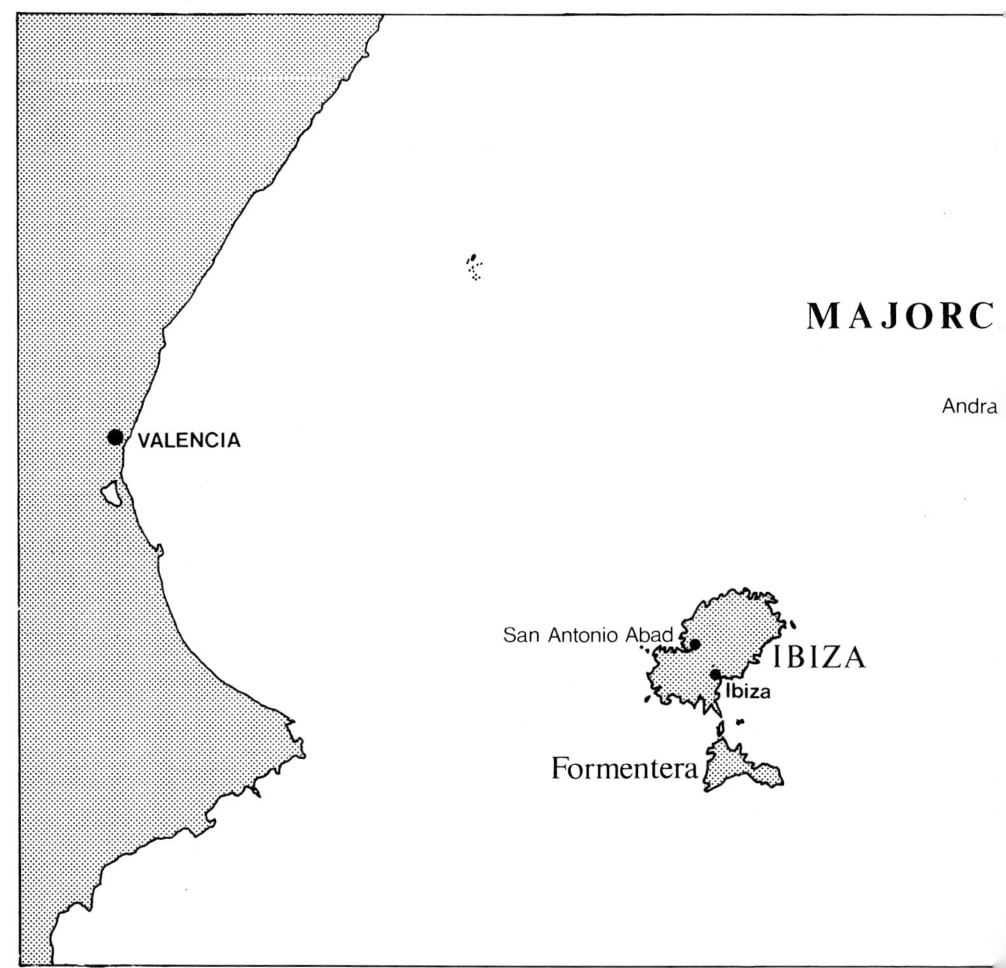

The Balearic Islands group is made up of sixteen islands, Majorca, Minorca, Cabrera and seven uninhabited ones, Ibiza, Formentera and four other islets.

You can tuck yourself away in some warm harbour here practically all the year round. Majorca attires itself in pink almond blossom from February and from then on until June the climate there is usually delightful; heat and holidaymakers are rather oppressive in the peak summer months although sea breezes help to moderate the former. September and October is delightful again. To the north, Alcudia, Cala Ratjada and

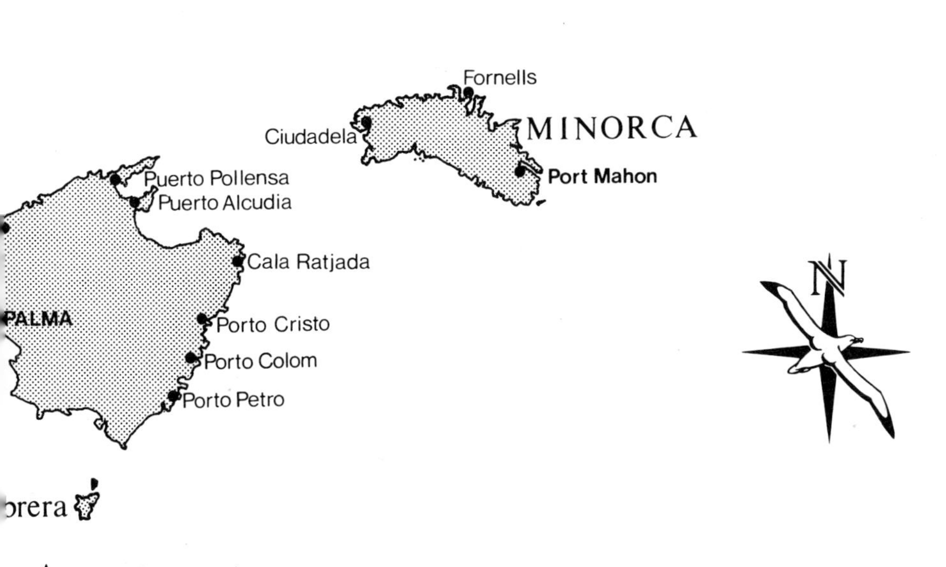

Average temperatures:

	Jan	Feb	Mar	Apl	May	Jun	Jly	Aug	Sep	Oct	Nov	Dec
MAX	58	59	63	67	72	79	84	84	81	74	65	59
MIN	43	43	47	50	56	63	66	68	65	58	50	47

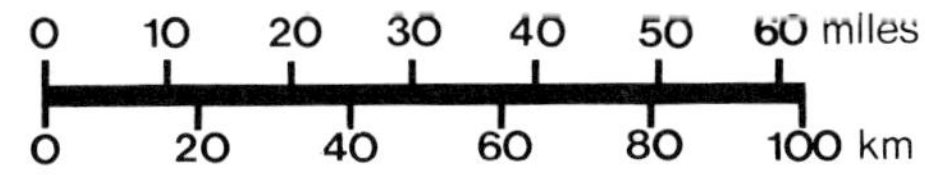

Pollensa are more exposed.

Minorca looks to France and Ibiza looks to Africa is a local saying; Minorca is certainly cooler and Ibiza certainly hotter than Majorca.

But with fifteen harbours you have plenty of choice and whatever time of year you take your boat to the Balearics you will be able to take your choice of a climate that suits you.

The Gothic Cathedral at Palma.

12 Majorca

Admiralty Chart 1317   (pop: 300 000)

Majorca is 60 miles across with a coastline over 200 miles long. It is 120 miles south of Barcelona and 130 miles west of Valencia.

Cruising around it you see mountains, flat plains, beaches, coves fringed with pine trees. Add to this the near certainty of sunshine, clear blue skies and seas and you have a perfect cruising ground.

Ashore your pink compatriots in their millions it seems are demanding stout-and-bit in preference to *sangria*, a knees-up in preference to *flamenca* but they come during the hottest months when you may prefer to be somewhere cooler.

HARBOURS OF MAJORCA
Palma
Porto Petro
Porto Colom
Porto Cristo
Cala Ratjada
Alcudia
Pollensa
Soller
Andraitx

Palma

This is undoubtedly one of the most beautiful and convenient harbours in the Mediterranean; if only so many other yachtsmen did not share this view it would be nautical paradise.

There are so many yachts here at all times that you have no difficulty in determining the yachts harbour locality; if you proceed to the inner mole, the Grand Mole, you will come to the pontoon moorings of the Real Club Nautico de Palma de Mallorca whose charges are:—

For the first two days	*per day*
up to 12 metres length	500 pesetas
up to 16 metres length	750 pesetas
over 16 metres length	1000 pesetas
thereafter:—	*per day*
up to 9 metres	125 pesetas
up to 10 metres	150 pesetas
up to 11 metres	175 pesetas
up to 12 metres	210 pesetas
up to 13 metres	250 pesetas
up to 14 metres	275 pesetas
up to 15 metres	300 pesetas
up to 16 metres	350 pesetas
up to 17 metres	400 pesetas
up to 18 metres	450 pesetas
over 18 metres	500 pesetas

You can also make arrangements to become what is known as a transient member, paying a lump sum and a reduced monthly payment. Details are included on the form that will be given to you on arrival.

Palma is an attractive city; you have only to step ashore and you are in it. If you like night life you can see it from your mooring. Splendid shopping, banks, drinks, museums, festivals, a fascinating old quarter with narrow winding alleyways to explore, a wonderful cathedral; everything you want is here.

But it gets oppressively hot in July and August and very crowded.

Palma Harbour.

Porto Petro
(Majorca)

Once in the bay you will see the mole; there is more water on the entry side than on the far side but there is plenty of depth in the middle.

Porto Petro is no more than a hamlet but it is quite attractive. The harbour is clean and quite charming; mostly it is quiet but there is a Club Méditerranée village there.

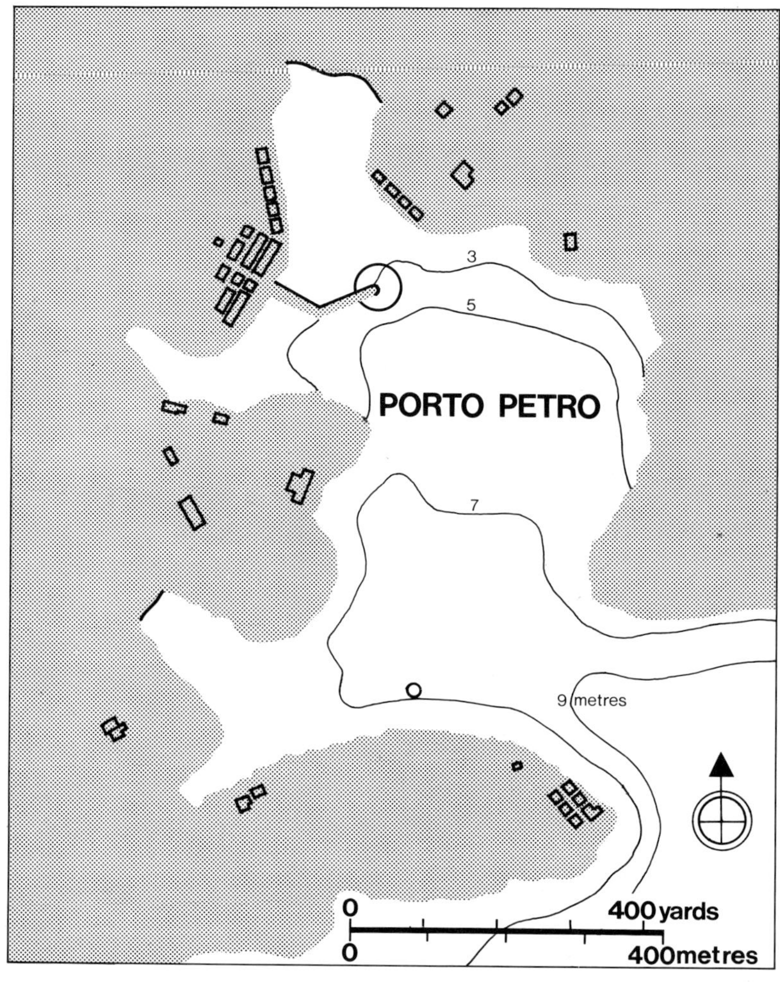

Porto Colom
(Majorca)

The entrance is shown on your chart; once inside the harbour make for the mole projecting towards you and tie up to the left of it as you go in.

The developers here seem to have tried to design the most hideous background to this intricate bay; the town simply sprawls around the shore, the gaunt headland appears to be littered with the drab shapes of hotels.

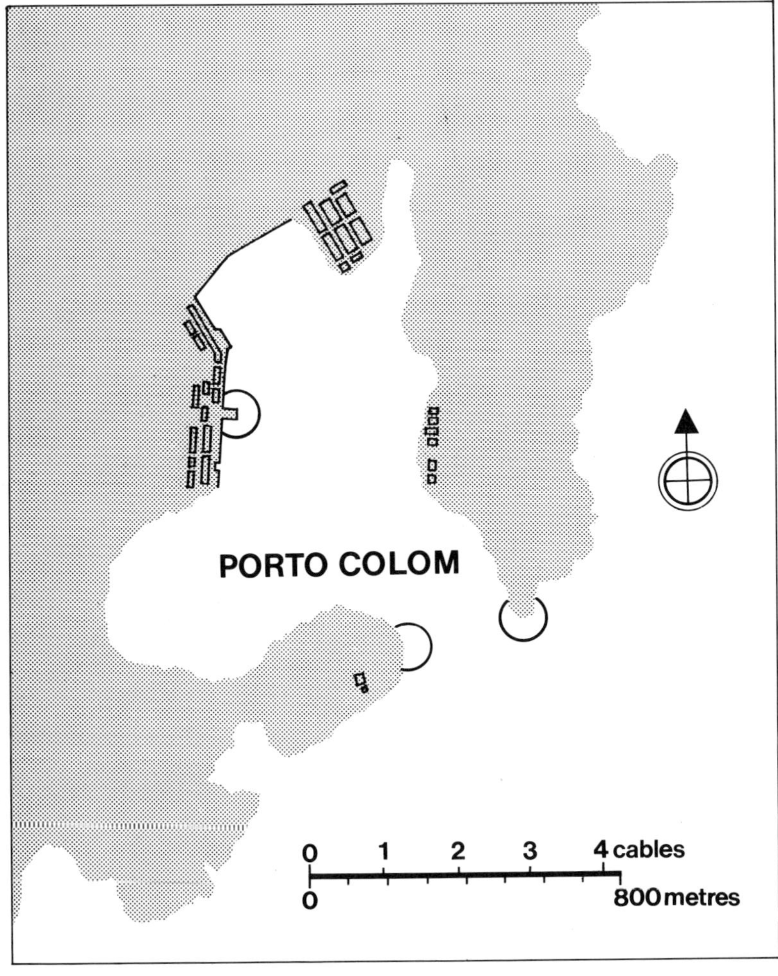

Porto Cristo
(Majorca)

As you round the Cabo de Morro you will see the mole ahead; when you round this the moorings come into view, moor alongside the quay beyond the fishing boats if there is room.

Being so near to Porto Colom it would seem that the same builders and developers must have created these two least attractive harbour areas in the island.

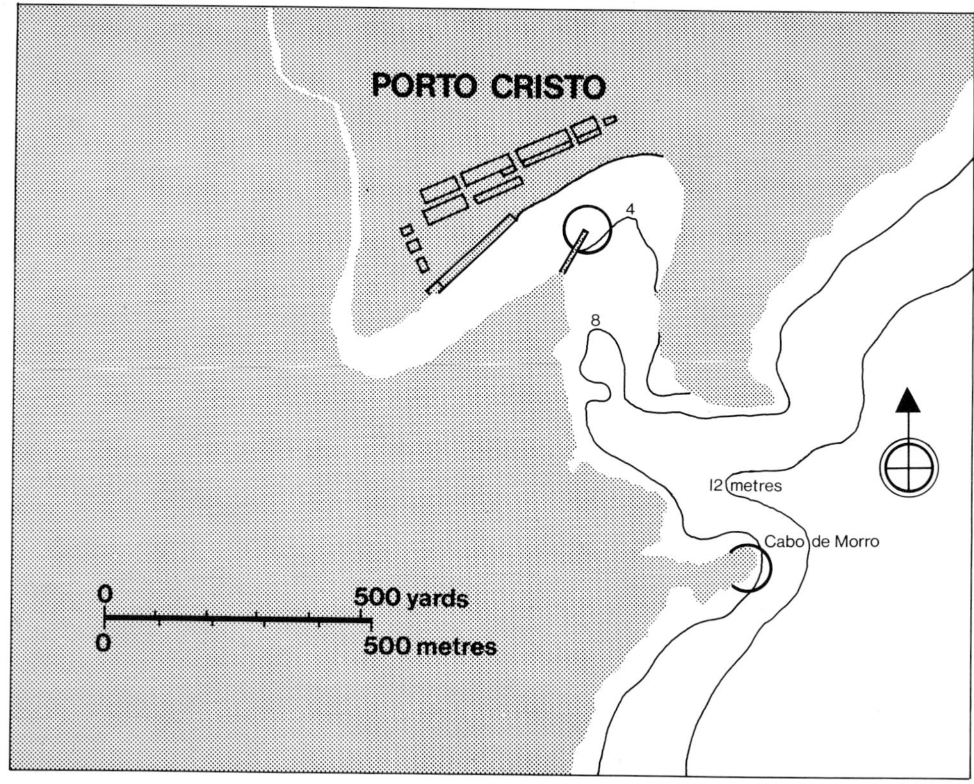

Cala Ratjada

(Majorca)

A fishing village, harbour, resort with a special character
and an appeal for all who fancy the simple life. It is too far away
from Palma and from the beaches to attract hordes of holidaymakers; therefore there is no night life. This attractive port has
retained the character of Majorcan life.

On rounding the mole keep to the right hand side of the
harbour, but do not secure to the quay immediately to your right
on going in for this is for the fishing boats and you will see yachts
moored just beyond.

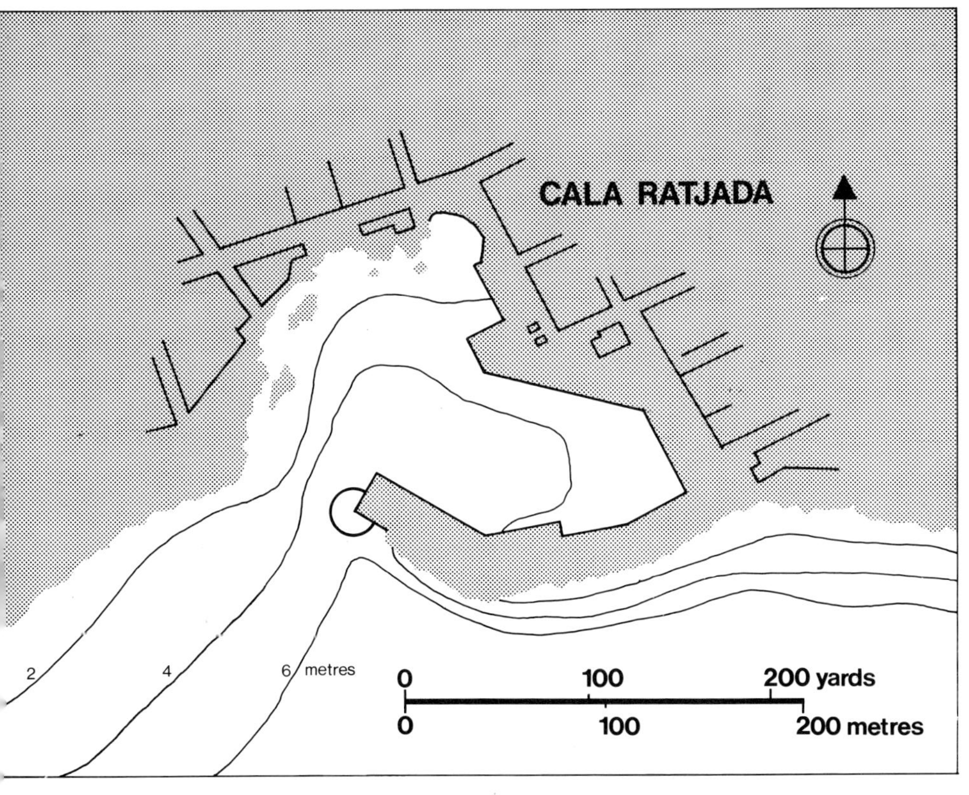

Puerto Alcudia
(Majorca)

Quite a pretty harbour with hotels lining the shore; its importance as a fishing port seems to be declining in favour of industry.

Situated at the end of a long beach the Puerto Alcudia does not attract holiday crowds and the town is a little way inland.

Pass the first mole on your right and proceed towards the second smaller one where you will see yachts moored.

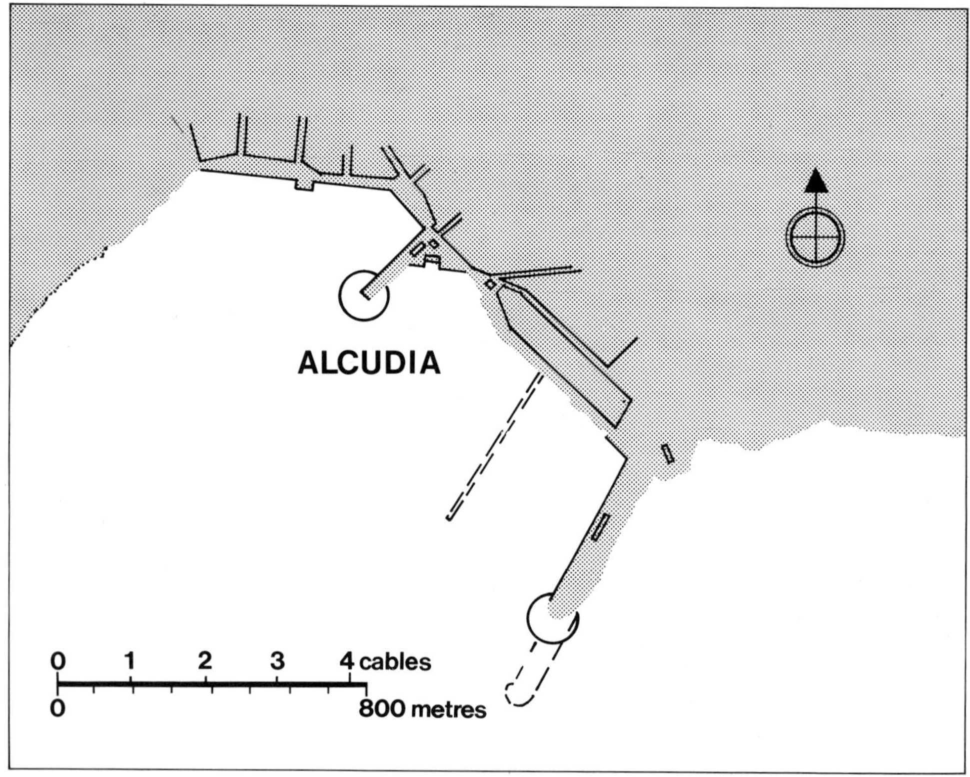

Puerto Pollensa
(Majorca)

Round the other side of Cape Formentor is the delightful little bay of Pollensa with the fishing port and harbour tucked away in the corner and the resort itself slightly inland.

Make your way across to the right hand side of the bay where you will see the two moles; entering between them you will find yachts secured by the left hand mole and fishing boats across to the right.

All shops are available and yacht repairs; for its size it is quite developed ashore with a promenade and lively atmosphere, hotels and night clubs.

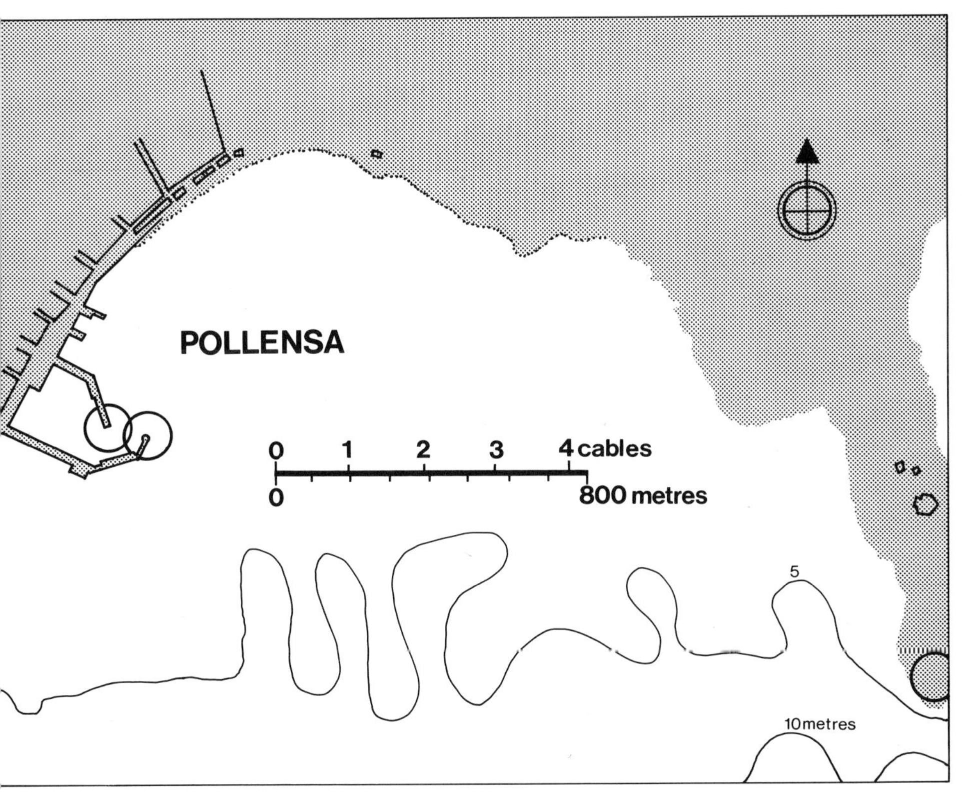

Soller
(Majorca)

Round the first mole on your left, past the second which you will see is reserved for naval craft, carry on round the fishing boats secured on the end of the third mole and you will come to the commercial and yacht harbour and slip.

This is an attractive harbour surrounded by mountains down which, in the winter months, squalls descend so that it is not a suitable place for a winter lay up despite its other attractions. It is quite a lively resort.

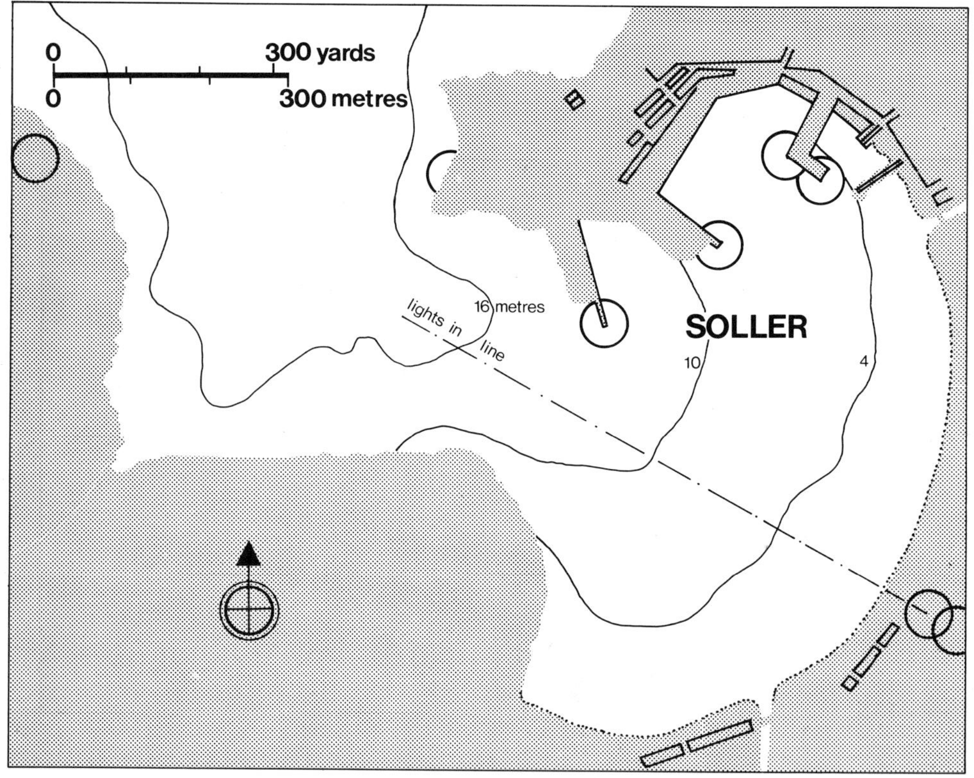

Andraitx

(Majorca)

A very snug little harbour, ideal for a long stay since it is well protected from all quarters.

Coming in you pass the breakwater on your left and make for the second, on your right, where you will see yachts secured.

There are shops to provide all basic needs.

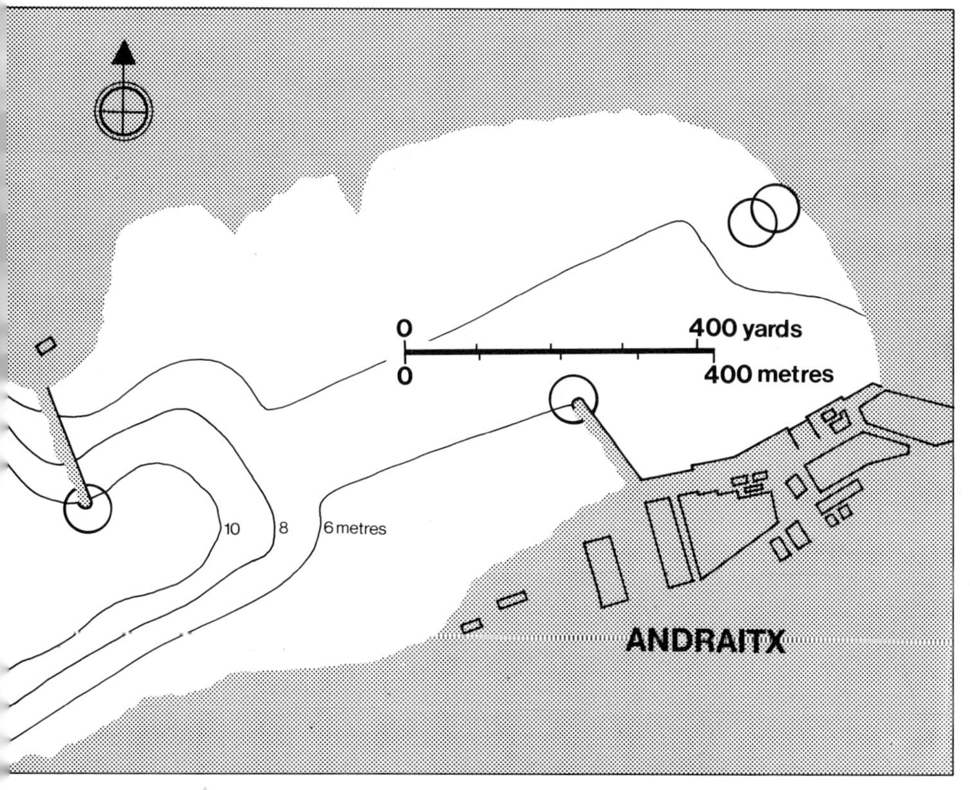

13 Minorca

Admiralty Chart 1317   (pop: 50 000)

Minorca is thirty miles long by ten miles wide approximately; it is not so crowded with holidaymakers, (apparently it would like to be), probably because its climate differs from that of Majorca, more probably because it is completely different from its larger sister island, without the colour and panache and the exciting goings on of Majorca.

It is surprising that Minorca is so much cooler but its changeable climate produces greener vegetation so that it resembles England in many ways.

It is really a summer place but in one respect it is superior for it possesses the best harbour in the Mediterranean . . . Port Mahon.

HARBOURS OF MINORCA
Port Mahon
Ciudadela
Fornells

The main harbour of Minorca is Port Mahon, one of the most beautiful natural harbours of the Mediterranean.

Port Mahon
(Minorca)

Your chart will guide you in to this beautiful harbour, past the islands, but there is plenty of water and you will see the big ship moorings, the naval moorings and the yacht moorings without any difficulty.

Port Mahon is the capital of Minorca and the most beautiful natural harbour in the Mediterranean. Despite its resemblance to an English country town it is very Spanish in its way of life.

Northerly winds seem to be blowing whenever we put into Mahon and we understand that you get winds from this quarter here for eight months in the year. But Lord Nelson must have been satisfied with this state of affairs and he probably steered his fleet on a northerly course on approaching to take what shelter he could; Mahon was his favourite Mediterranean harbour and you can still see the iron mooring posts and rings that his crews used to warp his ships in and out of harbour.

Everything you need can be obtained ashore.

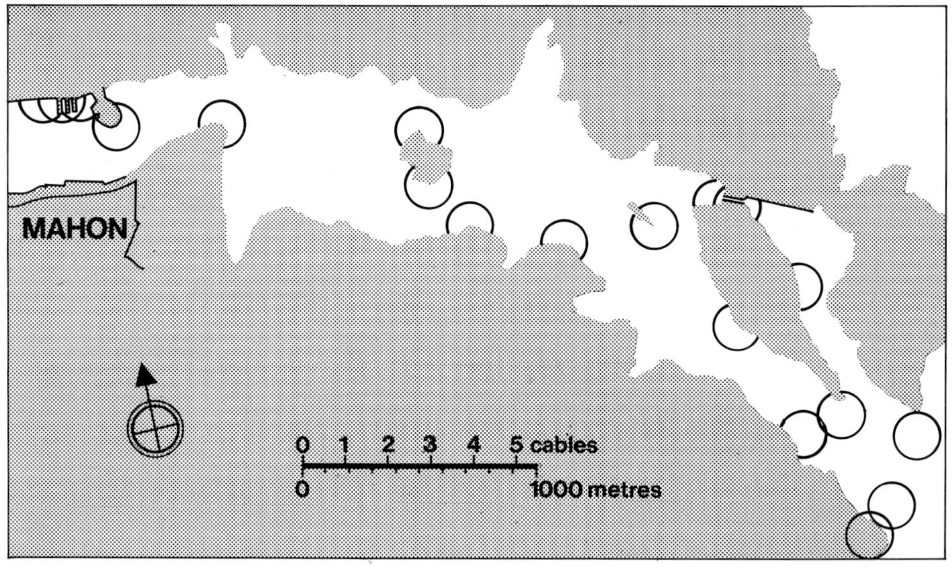

Ciudadela

(Minorca)

As you enter you should keep to the middle of the fairway where there is plenty of water; at the end of the bay, on your right, you will see the quays.

Ciudadela is a former capital of the island and it is an old place with Moorish and French influences to be seen. There are shops and most things that you need available but the surroundings are rather uninspiring.

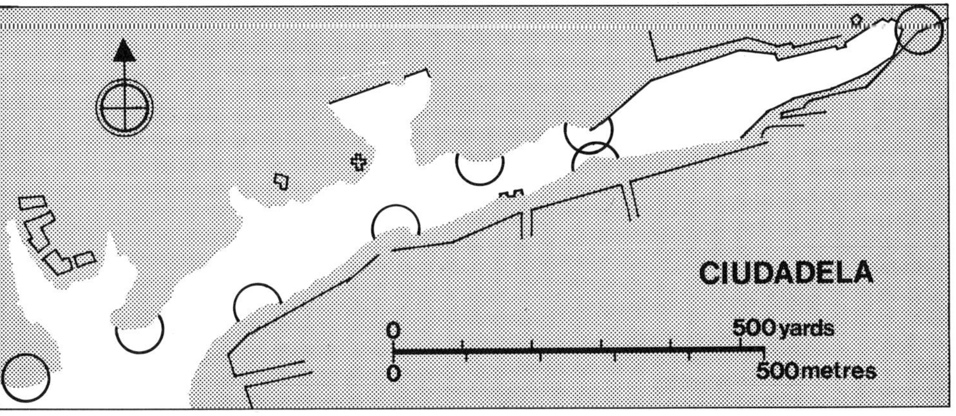

Fornells

(Minorca)

On entering the largish bay you will suddenly come across Fornells tucked away in to your right almost as soon as you enter. Proceed past the mole before seeking a place to secure.

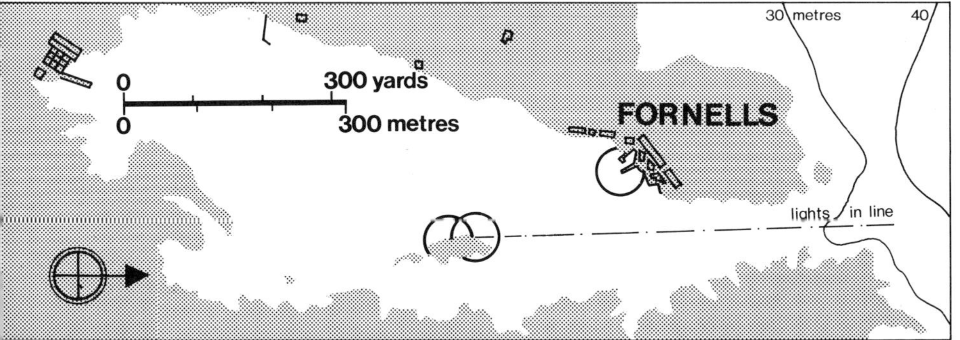

14 Ibiza

Ibiza attracts more holiday makers than Minorca mainly because it is the hottest of the three islands and with this goes colour; purple flowers against white houses, oleanders, olives and cactus in a background of rich red earth.

It is about twenty-two miles long by sixteen miles wide.

You can swim here at any time of the year; in midsummer you can watch your varnish peel for the sun burns really fiercely in Ibiza.

HARBOURS OF IBIZA
    Ibiza
    San Antonio Abad

The island of Ibiza is the hottest of the three main Balearic Islands. San Antonio Abad is the island's biggest resort.

Ibiza harbour has an enchanting maze of cobbled streets leading up from where the Barcelona steamer berths.

Ibiza

(Ibiza)

Enter between the moles and you will see the Club Nautico ahead; or you can secure on the inside of the first mole if you prefer.

Ibiza town rises steeply from the harbour through an enchanting maze of cobbled streets to the old walled city above.

Everything is here; you are right amidst the lively waterfront life, the gay cafes and bars and it seems like carnival time whenever the Barcelona boat leaves.

Apart from this the life here is pleasant and leisurely and you can sit for hours over drinks at terrace cafes with music.

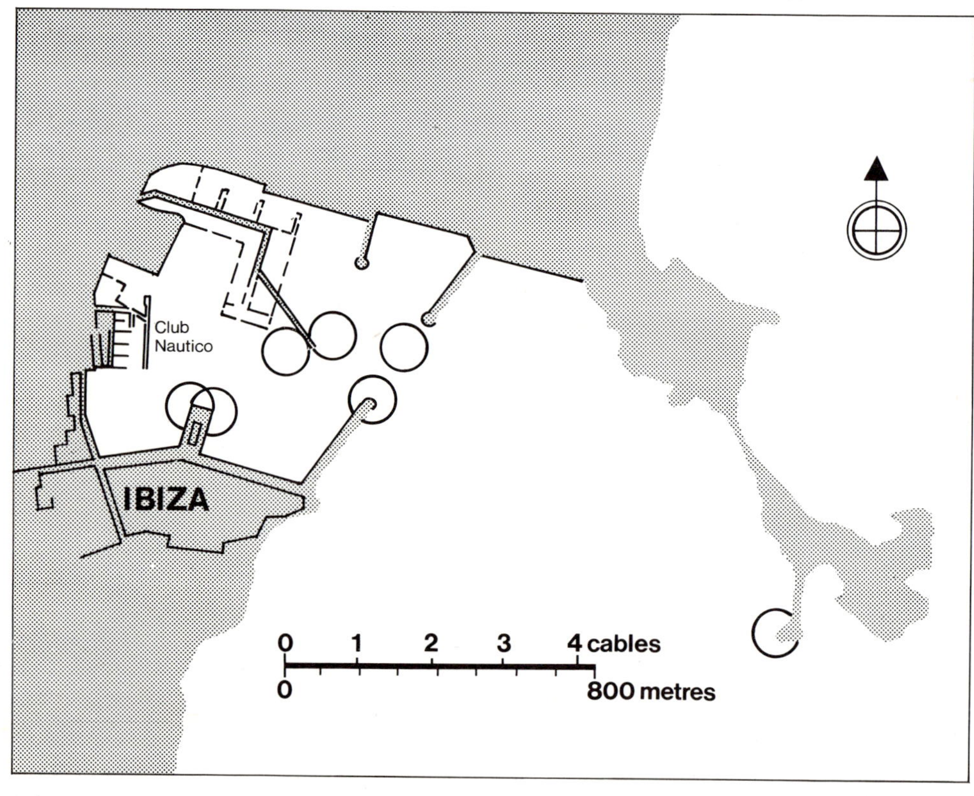

San Antonio Abad
(Ibiza)

On entering pass the mole and look for a place to moor, stern-to, on the other side.

San Antonio has grown rapidly from a small fishing harbour with a fortified church to become the island's biggest resort attracting numbers of British and German visitors.

There are bright little bars and restaurants, a good selection of shops, a gay central square, a large open air night club and a few discotheques.

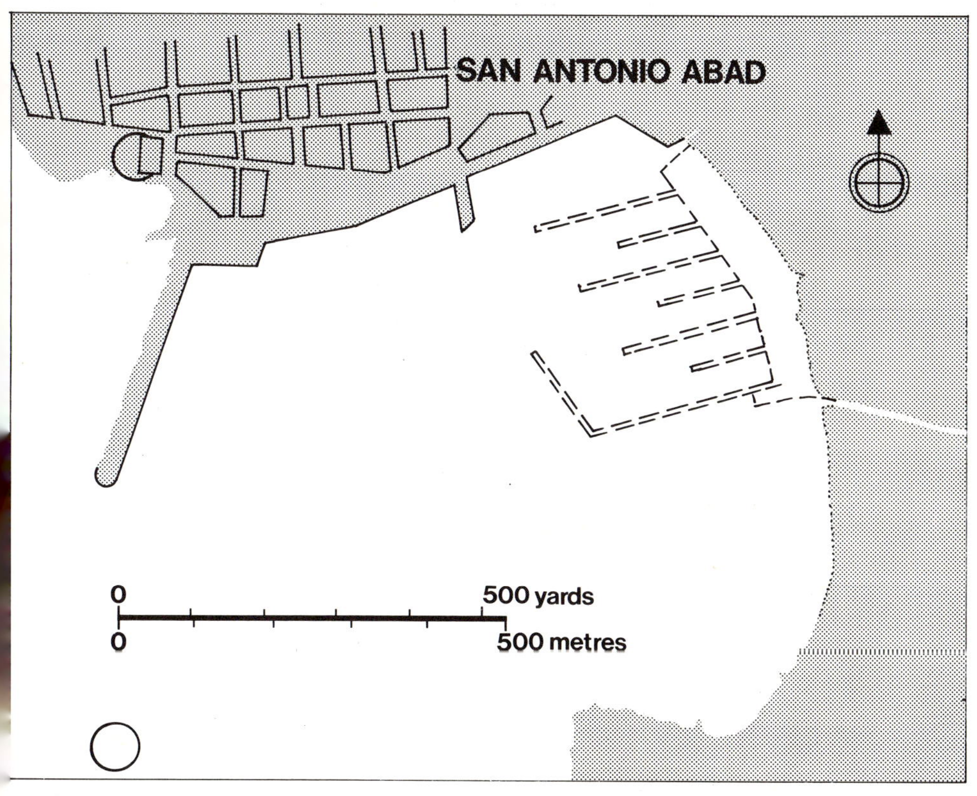

Formentera

Admiralty Chart 3276   (pop: 4000)

Formentera is about ten miles long but at one point is less
than a mile wide; there is a small port, Cala Sabina.

When you are in Ibiza you can follow the daily motor boat
the eleven miles to Cala Sabina if you have any doubts about
your navigation through the odd cluster of uninhabited islands that
lie on the route there.

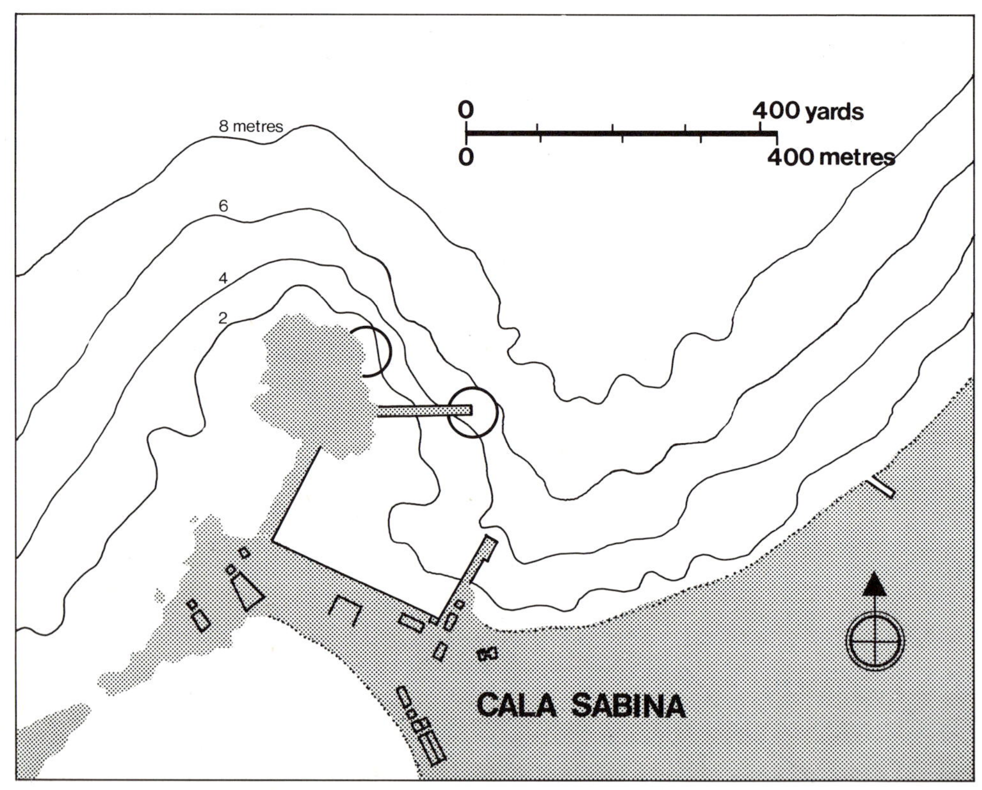

Cabrera

Admiralty Chart 1317

Cabrera is a rugged island belonging to the Military Authorities whose permission must be obtained to visit it.

The guidebook issued by the Spanish authorities states 'as a tourist resort Cabrera is NOT recommended'.

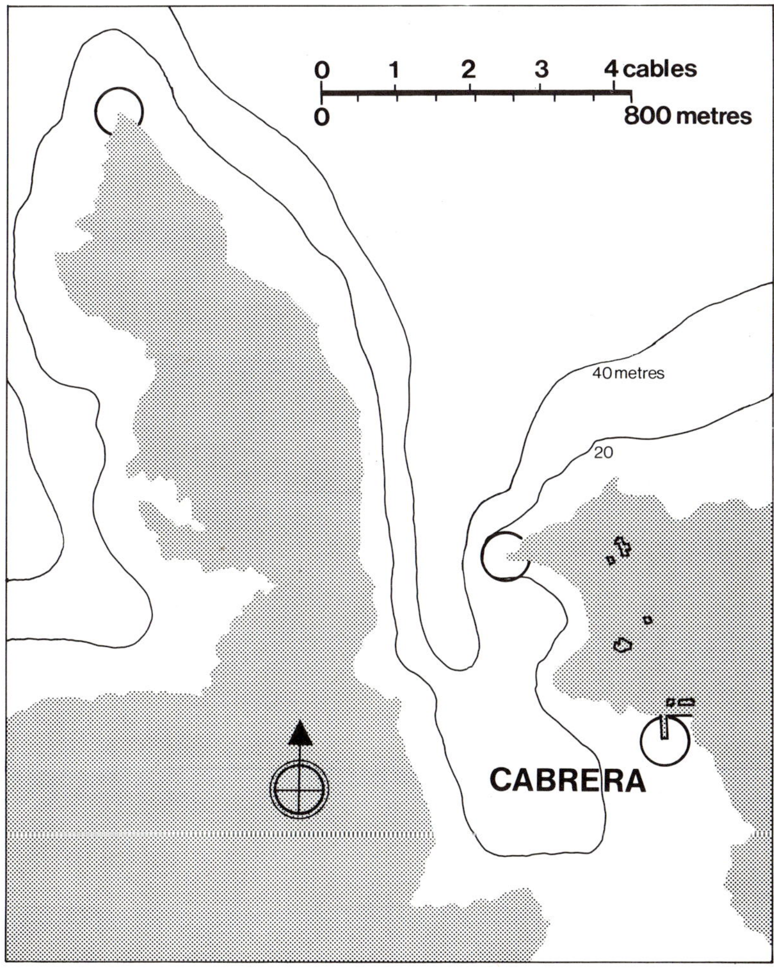

Index

Bilbao
MADRID
Almeria
Malaga
Estepona
Costa del Sol